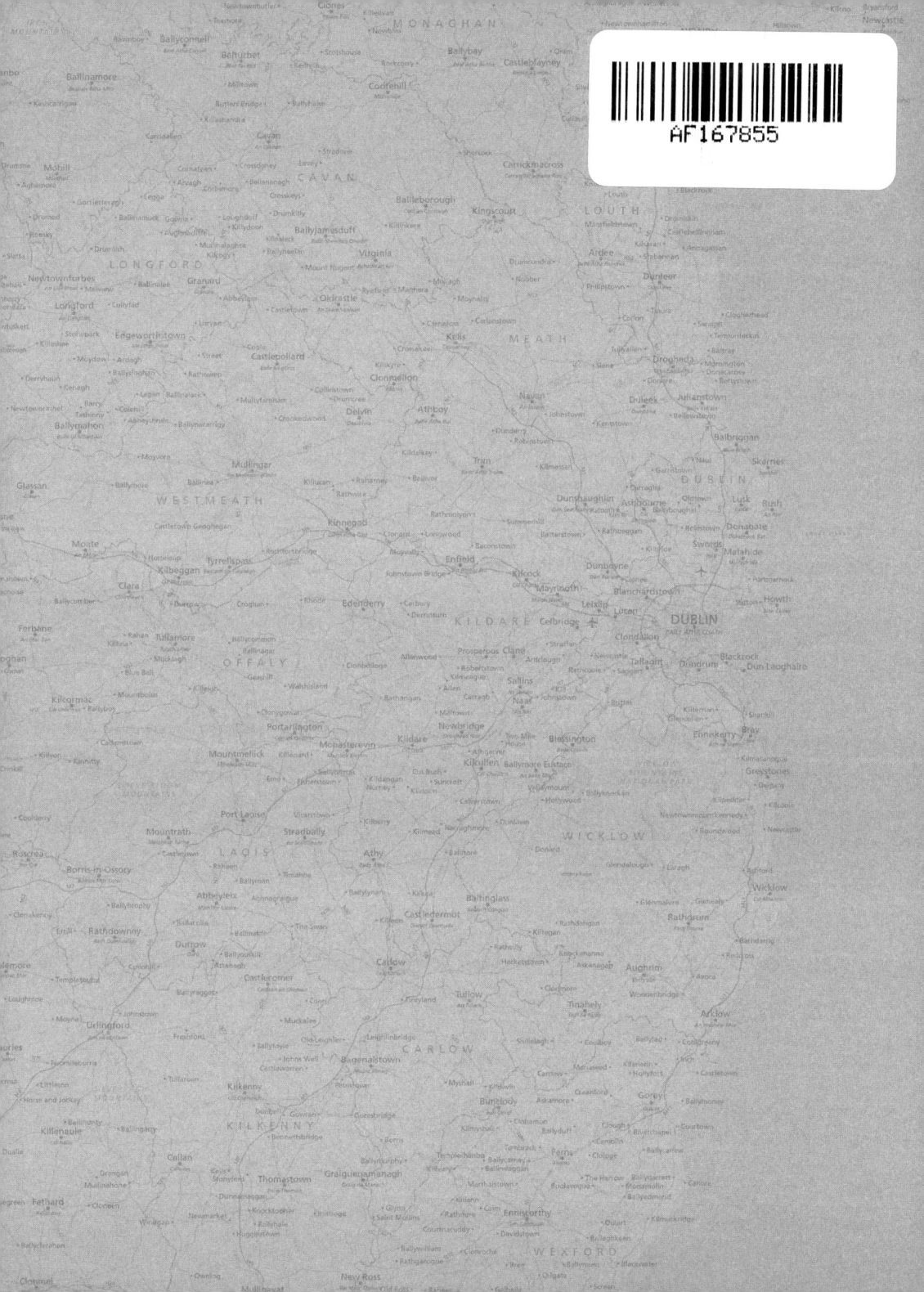

AF167855

GREAT IRISH ROAD TRIPS

Gill Books
Hume Avenue, Park West, Dublin 12

www.gillbooks.ie

Gill Books is an imprint of M.H. Gill & Co.

ISBN: 978-1-8045-8488-0

This book was created and produced by Teapot Press Ltd

Text by Nicola Brady
Designed by Tony Potter & Ben Potter

Printed in the EU

This book is typeset in Fields Display, Noto Serif and Noto Sans

To the best of our knowledge, this book complies in full with the
requirements of the General Product Safety Regulation (GPSR). For further
information and help with any safety queries, please contact
us at productsafety@gill.ie

Every effort has been made to ensure the accuracy of the trips in this book.
The authors and publishers accept no responsibility for any injury, loss or
inconvenience sustained by anyone using this guidebook.

A CIP catalogue record for this book is available
from the British Library.

5 4 3 2 1

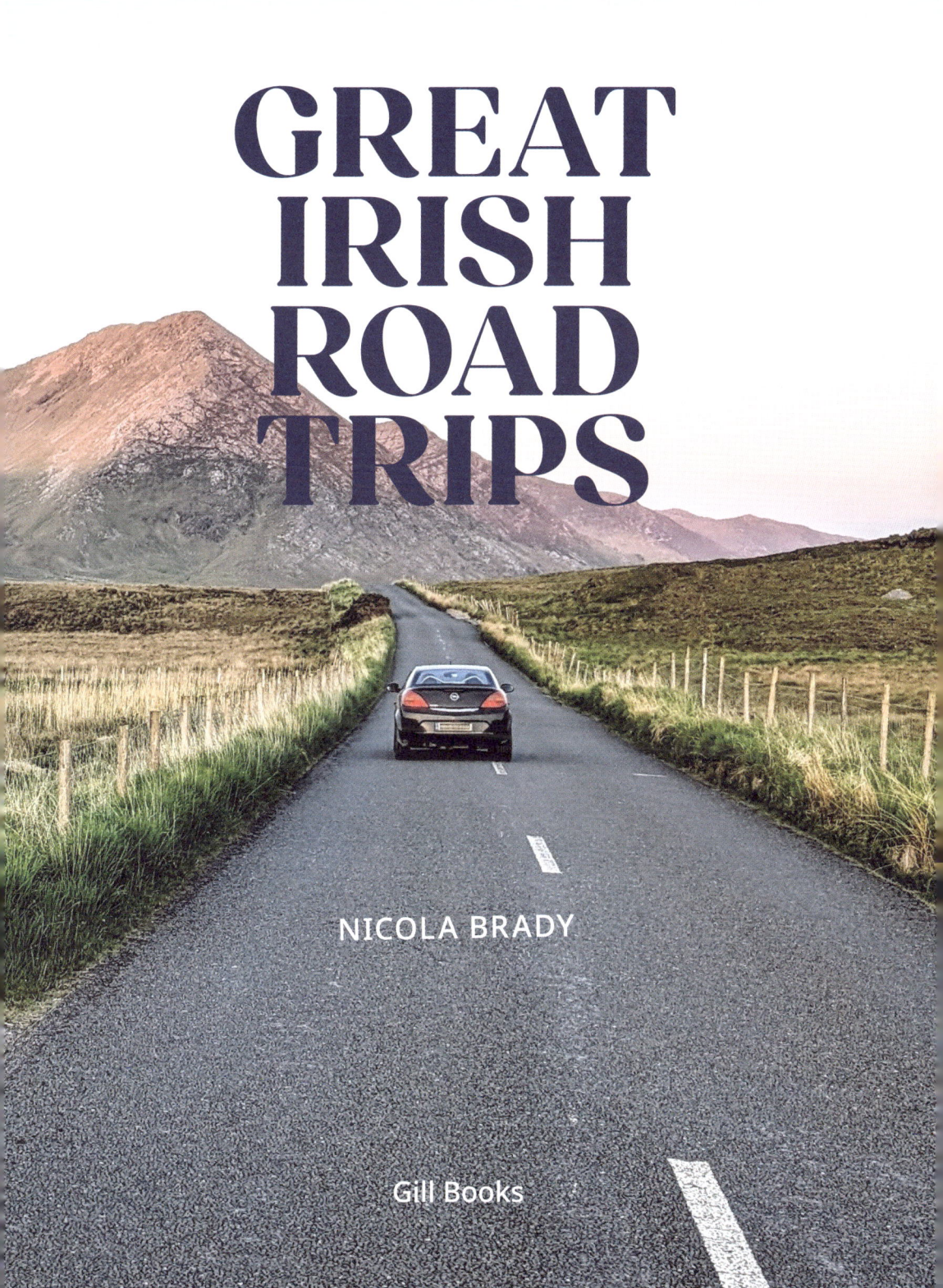

GREAT IRISH ROAD TRIPS

NICOLA BRADY

Gill Books

Contents

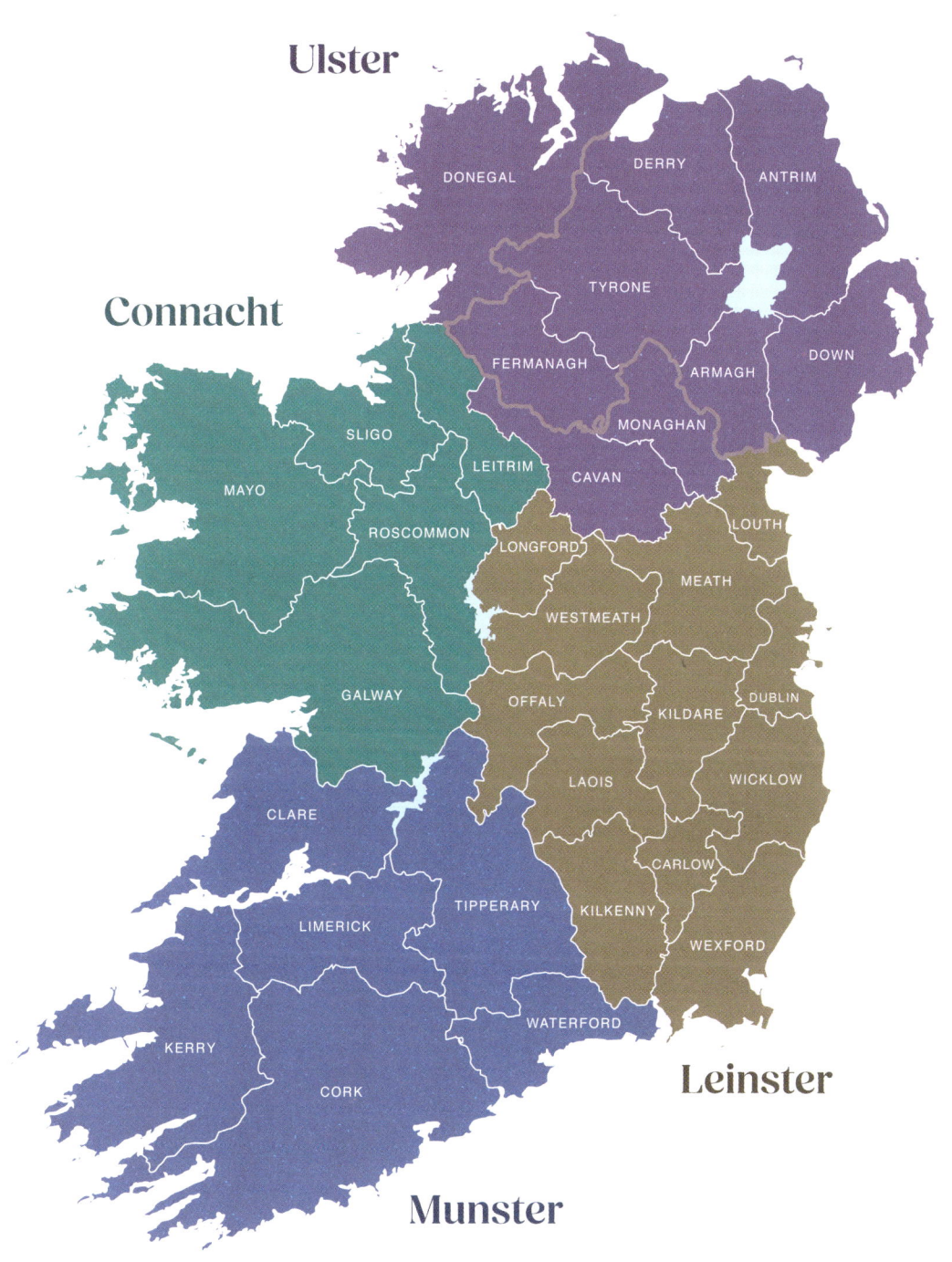

Ulster

Connacht

DONEGAL

DERRY

ANTRIM

TYRONE

DOWN

FERMANAGH

ARMAGH

SLIGO

MONAGHAN

MAYO

LEITRIM

CAVAN

LOUTH

ROSCOMMON

LONGFORD

MEATH

WESTMEATH

GALWAY

OFFALY

KILDARE

DUBLIN

LAOIS

WICKLOW

CLARE

CARLOW

TIPPERARY

LIMERICK

KILKENNY

WEXFORD

KERRY

WATERFORD

Leinster

CORK

Munster

Looking north along the Healy Pass
with Glanmore Lake on the left.

Introduction

One of the best ways to explore Ireland is on a road trip. Get behind the wheel and you could be driving along a mountaintop road that snakes along the edge of a cliff, or on a tiny boreen with grass growing up the middle and hedgerows almost touching the wing mirrors. It's a country where nondescript roads take you past centuries-old castles crumbling in a field, or alongside undiscovered neolithic tombs visited only by the local sheep.

And while many think of Ireland and imagine rolling green fields, there's actually great variety in the landscapes. Sure, there are plenty of the former, but there are also white sand beaches, tidal islands and medieval cities to explore, all within a relatively easy hop of one another.

As a travel writer, I've spent my career travelling the length and breadth of Ireland to report on the best beaches, secret spots and places to visit. I've included all of my favourites in this book, from the peaceful beauty of Strangford Lough to the gravity-defying rock formations off the North Mayo coast. But it doesn't matter how well you think you know Ireland – there's always something new to discover.

For geographic ease, we've divided this book into the four provinces of Ireland – Connacht, Munster, Ulster and Leinster (with a few crossovers, to keep things fun).

We start in Connacht, with road trips through Galway, Connemara, Mayo, Sligo and Leitrim, with a bonus bit of Donegal, too. This region is known for its wild, blustery landscapes, bulbous mountains, rich bogland and stunning shoreline, big wave surfing beaches to the north and pretty bays to the south. This is where you'll find Connemara, with its picture-perfect swathes of amber-hued hills, calm lakes with tree-covered islands and charming villages where you can finish the day with a pint and a platter of oysters. But you'll also get to explore the lesser-trodden pathways of Leitrim, the mountains of Sligo and the deeply beautiful Mayo, with its windswept cliffs and geological marvels.

From there, we move on to Munster, with itineraries for Kerry, Cork, Tipperary, Waterford and Clare. This is where you'll find the best-known spots – the Ring of Kerry, the Slea Head Drive and the start of Ireland's most famous road trip, the Wild Atlantic Way. But just because these routes are popular – so popular that taking them on in peak season may be a mistake – it doesn't mean they shouldn't be added to your bucket list. They're big hitters for a reason, after all.

In Ulster, we explore the counties of Monaghan, Cavan and Donegal as well as the entirety of Northern Ireland. Here, you'll find a treasure trove of striking scenery, from the lake isles in Fermanagh to the historic landmarks along the Antrim coast. It's also home to the Wild Atlantic Way's competition – the Causeway Coast. A drive up this stretch of shore will bring you to Victorian cliff paths, wobbly rope bridges and more than a few shooting locations for *Game of Thrones*, all along a stunning road that hugs the coastline.

And finally, we reach Leinster, exploring the countryside of Longford and the beaches in Wexford, with all the counties in between. You can drive through the national park in Wicklow, with its dramatic mountains and excellent hiking spots, or through the Boyne Valley, home to Ireland's biggest neolithic sites.

Every road trip in the book includes a map, but bear in mind these are designed as an aide memoire, so be sure to determine a route before you set off. This is particularly important when it comes to phone signals, which can get dicey in the further flung regions of the country. It's a good idea to download an offline version of a local map to your phone before you set off, or to use an old-fashioned paper map.

Each trip in this book has been planned with both beauty and practicality in mind. The driving distances are manageable, the routes are as scenic as can be without adding too much time to your journey, and all itineraries have time slotted in to actually enjoy the place, too. Because that is key – you want to make sure your road trip includes enough time out of the car, so you can really immerse yourself in the destination and make sure you're experiencing it properly. That can mean anything from a coastal hike to a leisurely lunch in a café.

But every trip is also designed to be customised to suit how you travel. You can pick and choose which elements you want to see,

and allow a bit of wiggle room to follow your nose. Whether it's checking out a sauna that you've stumbled upon, or heading to the pizza spot that someone recommended in the local pub, the best way to see Ireland is to give in to distraction and go wherever your heart takes you.

It doesn't matter how long you have to explore, either – this book gives you plenty of ideas for afternoon drives through quiet country roads, or epic road trips that'll take you to all of Ireland's best known sights.

Happy trails.

Panorama of Kylemore Abbey, a beautiful castle-like abbey in Connemara.

CONNACHT – Trip 1: 3 days
Galway to Connemara

If you were to close your eyes and conjure up the image of a quintessentially Irish landscape, it's likely you'd be thinking of a place just like Connemara. This pocket of land in County Galway ticks all the boxes when it comes to impressive scenery, with pristine beaches, rolling mountain ranges and lakes so calm they create mirrorlike reflections (when the weather is playing ball, that is). A drive through Connemara is one of the greatest pleasures you can have behind the wheel, and there are plenty of charming towns and villages along the way where you can make your base and tuck into some freshly caught seafood.

Need to Know

Duration: 3 days

Distance: 265km/165 miles

When to go: October, when the summer crowds have gone and the colours are at their prettiest

Start at: Galway

Finish at: Galway

The route

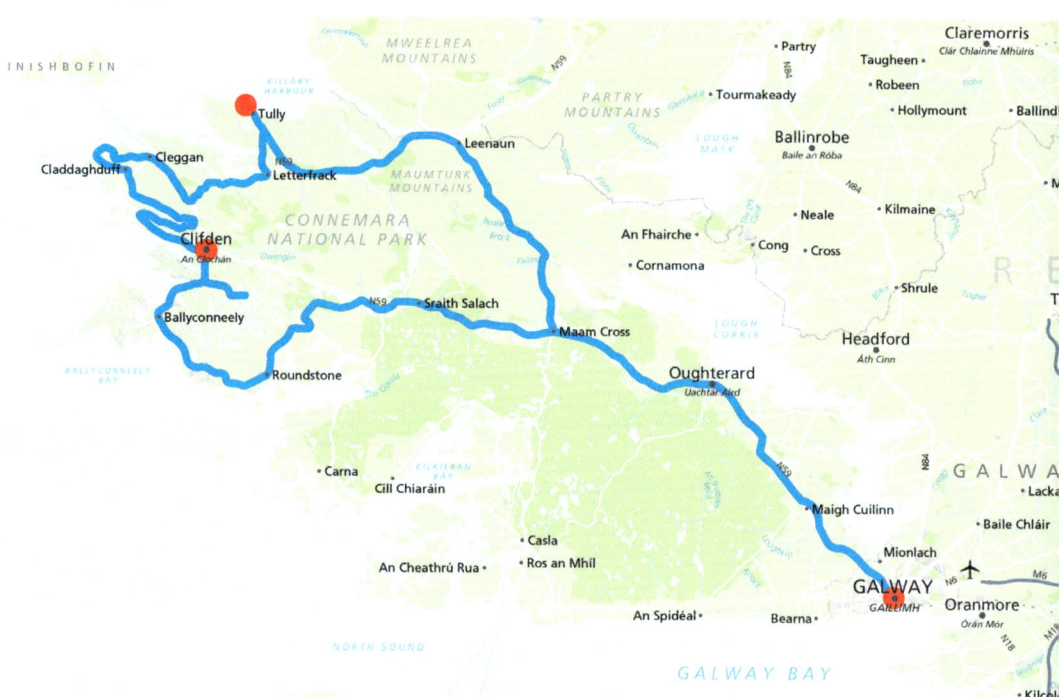

Quick view

Day 1: Galway to Cliffden

Drive from Galway to Clifden by way of pretty villages like Oughterard, mostly following the N59 and the Bog Road. Spend the night in Roundstone or the nearby Ballynahinch Castle.

Day 2: Cliffden to Renvyle

Explore the Sky Road, one of Ireland's most beautiful routes, and either drive to the tidal island of Omey or get the ferry to Inishboffin, before spending the night in Renvyle.

Day 3: Renvyle to Galway

Check out the lakeside Kylemore Abbey and Killary Fjord, before driving back down to Galway.

Day 1 – Galway to Clifden

Before you hit the road, spend some time exploring **Galway,** the lively little city known for its music scene, foodie culture and bustling weekend market. Take a stroll down Quay Street to hear the buskers play, then pick up a coffee in Coffeewerk + Press, which is part shop, part art gallery and purveyor of an excellent flat white. If you're in town on a Saturday, the streets around the cathedral are home to numerous market stalls, where you can buy homemade bagels, unique sushi rolls and decadent cheese toasties made outside the cheesemonger Sheridan's.

If you have the time, walk over the **River Corrib** to the **Westend,** a neighbourhood that has a cool community vibe, with excellent little book shops, pubs and places to eat – have brunch or a slab of cake in Kai before you hit the road.

While it's a great spot to explore in its own right, Galway is also the gateway to **Connemara**, where you can escape the city and quickly be among the kind of bulbous mountains, white sand beaches and picturesque lakes that make this corner of Ireland so mesmerising.

Shop Street, Galway city.

The initial stretch of the N59 isn't too exciting – think industrial estates and giant roundabouts – but things pick up once you reach the pretty village of **Oughterard.** Call into Sullivan's Country Grocer if you're feeling peckish (or want to pick up pillowy focaccia for a later picnic) then continue on the same road as it starts to weave through Connemara proper.

If you fancy a brief detour, turn left at Maam Cross and drive five minutes to **Screebe Waterfall,** a low-lying fall that flows over boulders and into **Lough Aughawoolia**.

Once you make your way back onto the N59, you'll be passing by scenic lakes and fields of boulder-strewn bogland, surrounded by gently rolling mountains. **Glendollagh Lough** is particularly distracting, so pull over if you can to drink in the views. Otherwise, continue beyond Recess until you reach **Pine Island,** the tiny lake isle with a line of tall trees running through its middle, with the **Twelve Bens** mountain range in the background. It's one of the most photographed spots in Connemara, with places to park up at the viewpoint, so pull in and snap a picture of your own.

Roundstone Bog.

Almost immediately, you'll need to turn off the N59 and onto the R341 to drive the **Bog Road** and through the **Roundstone Bog Conservation Area.** This looped road takes you into the pretty town of **Roundstone**, where you can call into the cosy pub O'Dowd's for a platter of oysters or a bowl of steaming chowder. If you have the time, hop out of the car to stretch the legs and walk around the harbour, too.

Just beyond the town, the beaches of **Dog's Bay** and **Gurteen** are two of the prettiest in Ireland, with glorious sandy beaches and dazzling waters – if the sun is shining, they could easily pass for the

Pine Island.

walk to the remains of the world's first trans-Atlantic radio station, built right here in 1907 and later destroyed in the Irish War of Independence. Nearby is the spot where Alcock and Brown crash landed in the bog in 1919, after being the first people to fly non-stop over the Atlantic. They survived, and the memorial honouring their feat is close by, too.

When you're finished, drive the short distance to **Clifden,** where you can make your base for the night.

Caribbean. If you're a sea swimmer, it's the perfect spot for a dip.

When you get back on the Bog Road, you can stop off at two key locations in Irish history. Make your way to the **Wild Atlantic Way Discovery Point** at Derrigimlagh and from there, you can

Day 2 – Clifden to Renvyle

Allow a bit of time in the morning to explore Clifden, taking a stroll through the town to call into the shops selling local tweed and Aran knits, before getting back into the car and setting off on one of the most scenic loops in Ireland.

Alcock and Brown's crashed plane in 1919.

Sky Road, Clifden.

The **Sky Road** may be short (about 15km in total) but it sure does pack a punch when it comes to scenery. Once you leave the town, you'll soon pass by **Clifden Castle,** which you can explore if it's open. Be sure to stick to the **Upper Sky Road,** and take your time, as it's fairly narrow and can get busy at times, particularly on summer weekends. Soon, this road will lead you to the Discovery Point stop, where you'll get some cracking views out over the undulating green fields that lead down to the Atlantic.

The great views continue as you drive over the headland, but when you get back to the N59 take a left to head towards **Claddaghduff.** The reason? It's one of the few islands you can drive to – if you get the tide times right, that is. But if you check (and double check)

that the tide is low, you can drive on the sand right to **Omey Island,** with wide sweeping beaches and medieval remnants. If you're nervous, you can always park up and walk over (and if you do drive, don't forget to triple check you'll catch the low tide on your return, too).

Omey Island beach road at low tide.

When you're back on solid ground, continue up and around the coast to **Cleggan,** where there's an island within reach that won't get your tires covered in sand. The crossing to **Inishboffin** only takes 30 minutes, and while you can't take your car with you, there's plenty to see on foot once you're on the island. Bear in mind that the ferry schedule usually means you'll spend most of the day on the island, so if you do want to head over, it's probably best to either skip Omey Island or go early (if the tides allow).

Back on the mainland, find the N59 and head to **Letterfrack,** then up north to spend the night in **Renvyle.**

Day 3 – Renvyle to Galway

Kick the day off with a walk on the beach in Renvyle, before heading back down to meet the faithful N59. From there, you're right on the outskirts of the **Connemara National Park**, and the information centre is just by Letterfrack. If you're a hiker, you can get out here and do one of the looped walks – there are shorter, easy loops and longer treks that take you up to the top of **Diamond Hill,** a fairly strenuous climb but one with beautiful views from the summit.

Back on the road, you'll soon find yourself at a particularly picturesque spot, **Kylemore Abbey.** This elaborate Victorian castle is right on the lakeshore of Pollacapul Lough, and is beautifully reflected in the water on calm, still days. Head inside, and you can find out all about the history of the building and the Benedictine nuns who call it home. Their walled gardens are spectacular, too.

From there, head back on the N59 along to **Killary Fjord,** a striking body of water that's the only glacial fjord in Ireland. It's impressive from the road, but you can get out on the water itself on a trip with Killary Fjord Boat Tours, which run mostly from April to October, but with some winter weekend sailings, too. You'll get a great view of the **Twelve Bens** and **Maumturk** mountain ranges, and may even see the local pod of dolphins playing in your wake.

When you continue, past the pretty waterside village of **Leenaun,** you'll take the R336 back down across the belly of Connemara until you reach Oughterard, ready to follow the same road back to Galway that you drove on day one.

Sunset over Killary Fjord, Connemara National Park.

CONNACHT – Trip 2: 2 days
Yeats County Loop

This corner of the country doesn't garner the same level of attention that Kerry and Connemara do, but the scenery is every bit as striking. There are huge lakes surrounded by deep green mountains, forest trails with boulders shrouded in thick moss, and epic walking routes that take you through beguiling countryside. And, even better, the fact that it's not on every tourist's trail means that you can often experience it without the hordes of visitors you may get elsewhere.

In both Sligo town and further into the county, you'll see one familiar face again and again. W.B. Yeats is the unofficial poster child for Sligo, and you can visit both his (supposed) grave and see the land that inspired his writing, all within a short distance. On this trip, you're not covering a huge amount of ground, but you'll need to allow plenty of time for roadside pit stops, hiking breaks and time spent drinking in those views.

Need to Know

Duration: 2 days

Distance: 148km/92 miles

When to go: June to August, when Lissadell House is open

Start at: Sligo

Finish at: Sligo

The route

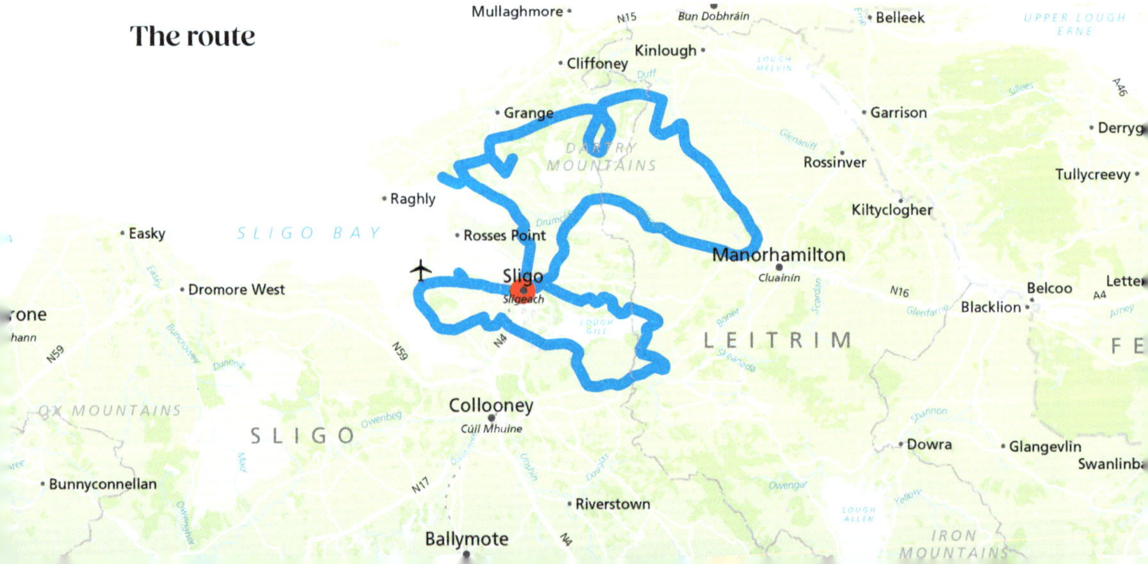

Quick view

Day 1: Take the N15 from Sligo out to Drumcliffe, before exploring Lissadell and Benbulben on the way out to the Gleniff Horseshoe. Stop off at Glencar Waterfall on your way back to Sligo.

Day 2: Start by exploring the tidal Coney Island before heading to Strandhill and Knocknarea, then loop down to Carrowmore Megalithic Cemetery. Drive around Lough Gill, stopping in Dromahair and Parke's Castle.

Sligo town.

Statue of W.B. Yeats in Sligo.

Day 1 – Sligo, Glenniff and Glencar

Start your day by exploring **Sligo** town, paying a visit to either one of the town's exceptional French bakeries for warm pain au chocolat, croissants or an artisanal baguette to tear into on the road. Le Fournil is right by the river, and the Lyons Café and Bakehouse is in the Henry Lyons department store, which has been a Sligo institution since 1878.

Just around the corner, the **Yeats Society Sligo and Hyde Bridge Gallery** is a must visit if you're a fan of the poet – there's usually an exhibition dedicated to his life and works on the go, as well as artwork displayed in the gallery, which is available to purchase. If you want to see more art, head a little further up the road to The Model, a contemporary gallery in a beautiful, light-filled space.

When you're ready to hit the road, leave the town and head out on the N15 towards Drumcliffe. If you're there on a Saturday, make a brief stop at the **Rathcormac Artisan Food and Craft Market**, where you can pick up locally made crafts, freshly baked goods and treats for later on.

Otherwise, you can make your first stop at the village church and the **grave of W.B. Yeats**. Now, there is some speculation as to whether this is in fact his final resting place – Yeats died in France in 1939 and his body was repatriated to Sligo in 1948, but French documents suggest the bones sent may not have been (all) his.

Either way, the grave is a tribute to the poet, his headstone inscribed with the epitaph: 'cast a cold eye on life, on death, horseman, pass by', words he wrote before he passed away. Nearby, there are also the remains of a sixth century monastery, and a high cross in the graveyard.

Continue briefly along the N15 before turning towards **Lissadell**. From June to August, **Lissadell House** is open for visitors and the tour is fascinating – you'll see the elegant interiors of this country house but also learn about its history. It was the childhood home of sisters Constance Markievicz and Eva Gore-Booth, whose signatures you can see scratched into a glass window in one of the drawing rooms. Yeats was enamoured of the sisters, and rightfully so – Markievicz was one of the leaders of the 1916 Rising and the first woman to be elected into the Dáil, and Gore-Booth was

a poet as well as a suffragist and activist.

You'll need to follow your tracks back to head to the next stopping point, the **Benbulben Forest Walk.** While Knocknarea is beautiful mountain, topped with the cairn of Queen Maeve, Sligo has not one but two distinctive peaks, and Benbulben is just around the corner. Marked with glacial track lines down its side, this flat-topped mountain looks a little like the Sugar Loaf, and the light and shadows play beautifully off its slopes.

If you want to get out and explore, park up at the forest walk car park, where you can stroll 5.5km through the woodlands at the foothills for great views of the mountain.

When you're finished, get back in the car to drive around the L3401 towards Benbulben's little sister, **Benwisken**. But your goal here isn't the mountain itself, rather the drive known as the **Gleniff Horseshoe**. This loop takes you into the belly of the glacial valley, driving deep into the crevices of the dark green Dartry Mountains. It's marginally better to take the second road you meet and drive the

Benbulben.

Gleniff Horseshoe.

loop in a clockwise direction, but it's usually blissfully quiet – just be sure to look out for walkers and cyclists, who follow the same 10km road as a hike or bike ride.

Along the way, you'll see old stone ruins, a herd of local sheep and a section of road called the 'Magic Drive' where, if you turn off the handbrake, you'll find yourself rolling uphill instead of down (just be cautious of others sharing the road, of course). You'll also see Diarmuid and Grainne's cave, where they hid from her jilted lover, Fionn MacCumhaill. It's beautiful from the road, but far too treacherous to climb – be warned that people have died trying to do so.

When you're back on the road, follow the route as it loops through the dramatic mountains until you reach the R280, skirting round the edge of Glenade Lough and heading south. Then, turn right on the N16 and head towards **Glencar Waterfall,** a beautiful spot that also served as inspiration for W.B. Yeats – check out 'The Stolen Child' to see it immortalised in poetry.

Hop out of the car and take a walk through the woodland to get the best view, and bear in mind it's at its best after a period of rainfall. When you're ready, get back in the car and drive over the undulating landscape back into Sligo town for the night.

Day 2 – Leitrim and Sligo

Before you start today's journey, you'll have to do a bit of legwork. Check the tide times for **Coney Island,** and if the low tides are in your favour then there's a fantastic drive to start your morning. From Sligo, head out towards Strandhill but take the right turn down to Coney Island. There, you can drive over the sands and follow the stone way markers until you reach one of the few Irish islands that's accessible by car (without a bridge). You'll want to triple check the times before heading out, and keep an eye on the timing so the tide hasn't risen before you need to drive back, but it's a charming little island well worth the effort.

Glencar Waterfall.

When you're back on solid ground, continue to Strandhill, stopping first at the **Knocknarea** car park to climb the other of Sligo's distinctive peaks. With a wooden boardwalk weaving through the forest and steps up to the summit, it's not a challenging climb, though it is fairly steep – allow about 1.5 hours to get up and down. Along the way, there are QR codes you can scan to listen to interesting snippets about the history and folklore of the mountain and Queen Maeve, whose giant tomb gives the mountain its distinct bulbous summit.

Down at the bottom, follow the road into **Strandhill** and stop off for a coffee and a bite to eat at Shells Café, or a seaweed bath at Voya if you have the time – these old cast iron tubs are filled with freshly harvested seaweed and seawater, and will leave you feeling brand new. If you didn't manage to get out to Coney Island but still fancy a walk on the sand, head out along the paths by the sand dunes towards **Killaspugbrone**, to find a peaceful little bay and deserted graveyard.

Drive out of Strandhill and along the southern edge of the peninsula until you reach **Carrowmore Megalithic Cemetery**, where you can explore tombs that are more than 6,000 years old.

Now it's time to drive around Lough Gill, a highly underrated route that's one of the best drives in the country. You'll swing by Slish Wood (getting out for a walk through the woods if you'd like) and follow the road to **Dromahair**, taking a detour if you want to see the Lake Isle of Innisfree, 'where peace comes dropping slow' in the words of Yeats, who wrote a poem dedicated to the island.

Stop off in **Dromahair**, calling into Leitrim's oldest (and possibly most charming) pub Stanford's, for a cup of tea or a 0.0 pint if you need a breather. From there, the road around the lakeshore is stunning, skating right on the edge of the water with the mountains rising in the background. There are a few places to pull in and take in the view from the layby, so do so in order to make the most of the setting.

Carrowmore Megalithic Cemetery.

If you have the time, call in for a self-guided tour of **Parke's Castle**, a seventeenth-century structure built right on the edge of the lake, that looks a little like a miniature Hogwarts. Be sure to take a walk on the grounds too, to get a great vantage point of the water.

From there, the road continues along the lake shore before cutting inland and leading you back into Sligo town.

Parke's Castle.

CONNACHT – Trip 3: 3 days
Best of Mayo

The Wild Atlantic Way takes in all that's great about the Mayo coastline, and it's one of the most scenic stretches of the drive. However, while the shoreline is beautiful, there's also plenty to see inland, from the charming villages and country pubs to huge lakes and romantic, crumbling ruins. This three-day route showcases the highlights of the county, from the wilds of Achill Island to the wide expanses of the Dark Sky Reserve.

Need to Know

Duration: 3 days

Distance: 327km/203 miles

When to go: May, when the wildflowers are in bloom

Start at: Castlebar

Finish at: Mulranny

The route

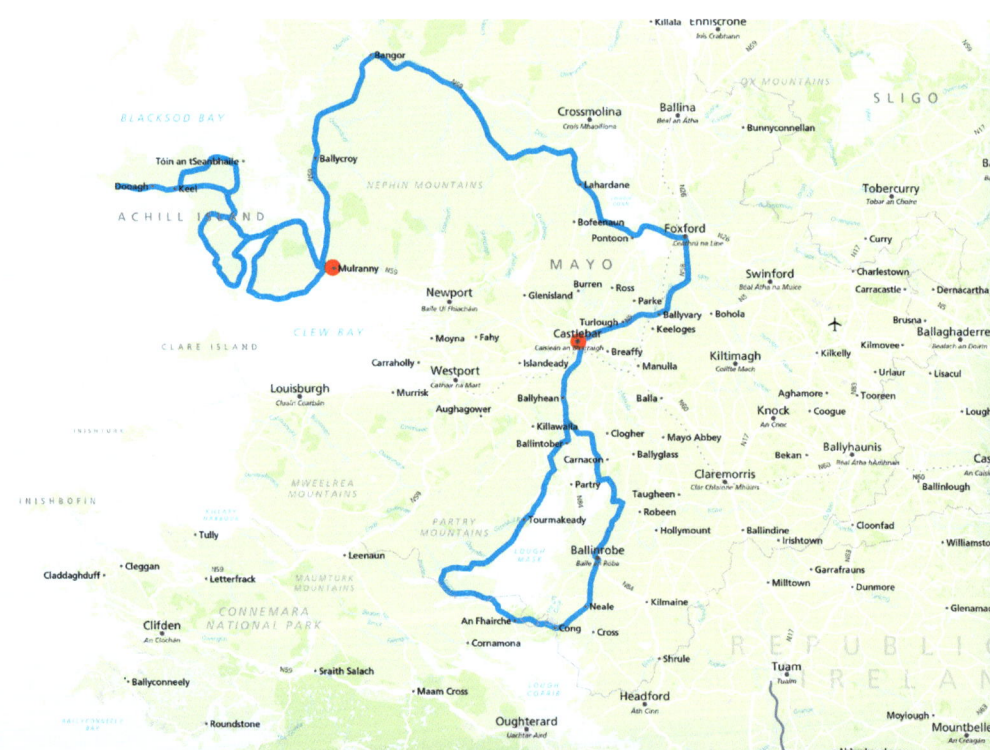

Quick view

Day 1: Head from Castlebar down to the historical sites of South Mayo, from Ballintubber Abbey and Moore Hall to the lake views around Tourmakeedy.

Day 2: Take the long route from Castlebar to Mulranny, seeing the Nephin Beg mountains, top museums and the Dark Sky Reserve along the way.

Day 3: Drive the Wild Atlantic Way all around Achill, taking in the wild, rugged beauty of Ireland's biggest island.

Day 1 – Cong, Toormakeady and Ballintubber

Start your day in **Castlebar**, with a stroll along the shores of **Lough Lannagh**. The full 7.3km long greenway leads you all the way out to Turlough and the National Museum of Ireland, but for this morning you can simply walk a little stretch out and over the water, turning around when you feel like heading back.

When it's time to hit the road, head out of Castlebar on the N84 until you reach **Ballintubber Abbey**. This active church is surrounded by the ruins of the 800-year-old abbey, and you can learn all about its history (and its connection to the Pirate Queen, Grace O'Malley) on a guided tour. Afterwards, be sure to wander the grounds to see the ancient carvings, sculptures and Celtic symbols dotted around. There's a great view of Croagh Patrick in the background, too – this church is the start point for the Tóchar Phádraig, a pilgrimage trail that leads all the way to the top of the Reek.

Continue on the L1709, skirting the edge of Lough Carra, until you reach **Moore Hall**. This grand house was built in 1792 but burnt down in 1922, and is now

Ballintubber Abbey.

a skeletal shell of a building, albeit one that's rather striking. The exterior remains in remarkably good shape, with thickets of ivy growing around the grey walls, around the stone pillars and through the empty windows. While you can't go into the house, there are beautiful walking trails around the estate, which are dotted with wooden chainsaw art of woodland creatures. You can walk through the old tunnels and see the structures that are now protected, thanks to the rare bats that live inside.

Back on the road, head south towards **Ballinrobe**, passing over the pretty **Carr's Bridge** along the way. If you fancy a brief detour, you can turn off to drive towards **Caher Pier** or **Inishmaine Abbey**, both on the shores of Lough Mask, and about a 13-minute drive from Ballinrobe.

Otherwise, continue on the road to Cong, famous for two things – classic movie *The Quiet Man*, starring John Wayne and Maureen O'Hara and filmed in the village, and Ashford Castle, the luxurious hotel on the shores of Lough Corrib. Stop here for lunch, either in a café in Cong or in Ashford Castle itself, where non-residents can eat in the beautiful Drawing Room if you book in advance.

Once you leave Cong, you'll be ping-ponging over and back across the Mayo/Galway border, weaving along the edge of Lough Mask before crossing the Ferry Point Bridge to head towards **Toormakeady**. Be sure to take the L16005 to make a brief stop at the **Lough Nafooey Lookout**, which gives you a great view out over the Galway lake.

The drive to **Toormakeady** is a stunner, and just a two-minute drive off the road you'll find a beautiful waterfall and woodland, which was once owned by the landlord George Moore, of Moore Hall. Take a brief walk to get to the impressive falls.

Afterwards, follow the road north until you reach the N84, and retrace your route back up to Castlebar.

Moore Hall.

Toormakeady.

Reflection of the Nephin mountain range overlooking Lough Feeagh near Furnace, County Mayo, in the Wild Nephin National Park.

Day 2 – Castlebar to Mulranny

Start the day with a visit to the **National Museum of Ireland** at Turlough Park, less than a 10-minute drive from **Castlebar**. Combining a beautiful Victorian gothic building and modernist galleries, the museum is set on a rolling green estate and delves into the history and sociology of Irish life.

You'll get a glimpse into what life was like in rural Ireland in the nineteeth-century, with homesteads set up to help set the scene – keep an eye out also for their original carved Samhain turnip, an early prototype for the pumpkins we now see on Halloween.

Follow the N5 before turning off at the N58 for another lesson in Irish history, this time at the **Michael Davitt Museum**. This tiny museum is in the village of **Straide**, where Davitt was born during the Famine. Throughout the space, you'll learn of the activist whose work was pivotal in the creation of land reform and the Land League, as well as the formation of the Women's Land League. You'll see

his handwritten letters, postcards and his armchairs, and his grave is at the back of the museum, in the remains of **Straide Abbey**.

Further up the road, you'll pass by the remains of **Ballylahan Castle** to the right, before reaching the pretty village of **Foxford**. This name is known all round the world thanks to the woven items made right here, and the **Foxford Woollen Mills** is well worth a pit stop. You can take a tour of the mills themselves and learn all about the history of the operation, before browsing their collection of herringbone blankets, throws and homewares and sitting in the (excellent) café for a cup of coffee and a slice of homemade cake.

Afterwards, head west, crossing the **Pontoon Bridge** that marks the space between Loughs Conn and Cullin, for a great view over the water. From there, the drive takes you up and around the beautiful bogland of Mayo, through the foothills of the **Nephin Beg mountain range**.

Mountain landscape in Achill, Great Western Greenway trail.

Your next stop is the **Ballycroy Visitor Centre**, in the heart of the **Wild Nephin National Park**. Open from February to November, the centre showcases the depths of wildlife found within the bogland in the park, but it also serves as the hub for the Mayo Dark Sky Park. Keep an eye on their schedule, as they often run guided stargazing sessions, film screenings and astrophotography events. But you can also come at any time, park up and do your own gazing at the pure, unpolluted night sky.

From there, it's about a 20-minute drive to **Mulranny,** where you can stay for the night. If you arrive with enough time to spare, you can check out the final (and most scenic) stretch of the **Great Western Greenway**, on a 14km cycle that leads you all the way to **Achill Island** on a stunning offroad trail.

Day 3 – Achill Island

Before we had the Wild Atlantic Way, **Achill** had the **Atlantic Drive**. This 39km loop weaves around the **Currane Peninsula** before crossing onto Achill, taking you past some spectacular coastal scenery. Kick things off by leaving Mulranny and turning left to follow the Coast Road. This waymarked trail will lead you first to **Doaghbeg**, a Discovery Point where Corraun Hill rises behind a wild beach.

From there, you'll follow the coastal road until you reach **Spanish Armada Viewpoint**, with a plaque dedicated to those who lost their lives when the ship sank in Clew Bay in 1588. You'll have great views of Achill and the nearby **Clare Island**, as the road follows the edge of the peninsula (you'll finish the rest of the loop later) and leads you to Achill itself.

Mulranny Bay.

The largest of all the Irish islands, Achill is also one of the easiest to access – you simply drive over the bridge. Once you're there, there's a huge amount to see and do in a day. When you've passed **Achill Sound**, follow the Wild Atlantic Way signs to the left, to follow the waterline all around the island. You'll pass by the crumbling remains of **Grace O'Malley's Tower House** before you reach **Cloughmore**, a gloriously rugged stretch of shoreline where you can also catch a ferry to Clare Island on some days (though more regular services run by Roonagh, near Louisburgh).

Here, you can also see the spot where they built a temporary pub for *The Banshees of Inisherin*, set on a fictional island but filmed mostly on Achill. There are a few movie locations to be found on the island, including this road itself. You'll reach one of the most iconic locations (both in the movie, where Colm's cottage was set, and on Achill itself) after you pass through **Keel** village and reach **Keem Bay**, a hugely picturesque beach with a curved, white sand shore, clear waters and mountains all around. You'll likely meet a few of the native straggly sheep along the way, who cling precariously to the grassy outcrops on the side of the road, but remember – on the island, they have right of way.

This marks the end of the Wild Atlantic Way road, so turn there and head back to follow the northern shore, taking you past the **Deserted Village** and up to the blustery tip of the island, before heading back over the bogland and back towards Achill Sound. From there, your route back to Mulranny will take you on the rest of the Currane Peninsula, following the calm waters with incredible views of Claggan Mountain.

Keem Bay.

Achill Island.

CONNACHT – Trip 4: 2 days
Ballina to Fanad

Some of Ireland's best scenery can be found in the blustery northwestern corner of the country. But while the coastline from Mayo up to Donegal is spectacular, the places you'll find inland are just as alluring. On this road trip, you'll weave in and out of the Wild Atlantic Way, but take in some of the best scenery that Sligo and Donegal has to offer, whether that's the wave-battered beaches of Mullaghmore and Bundoran, or the peaceful, dramatic mountain ranges in and around Glenveigh National Park.

Need to Know

Duration: 2 days

Distance: 291km/181 miles

When to go: Autumn, when the leaves are turning

Start at: Ballina

Finish at: Fanad

The route

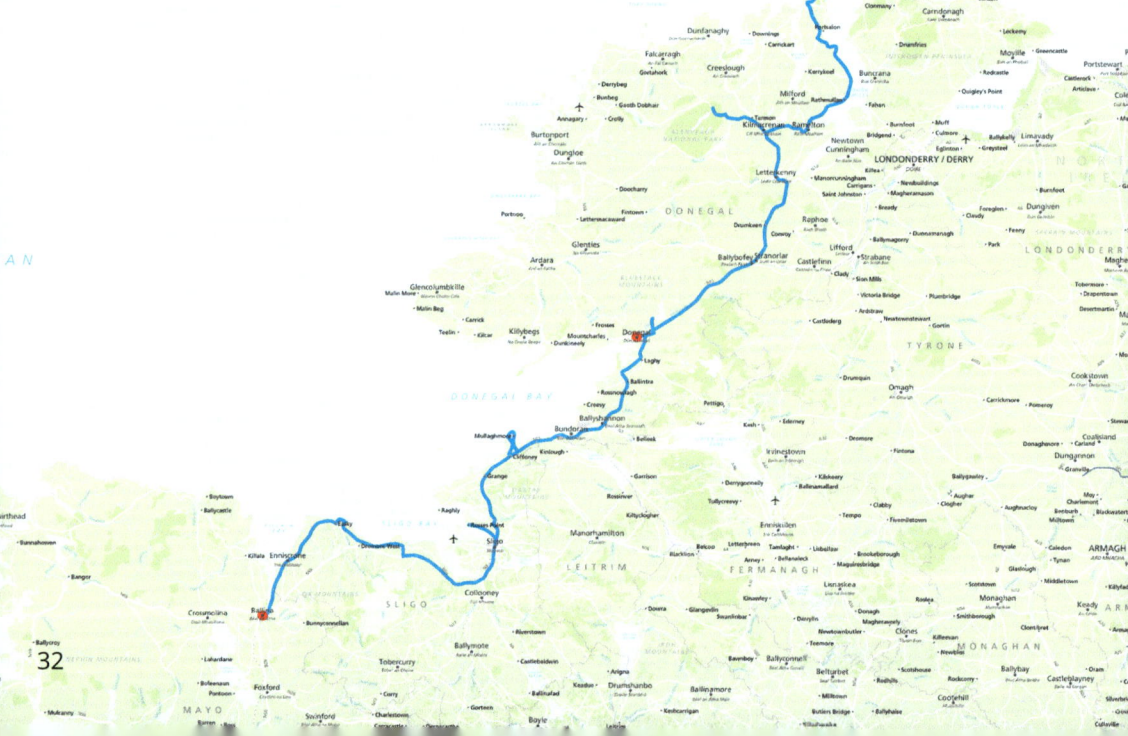

Quick view

Day 1: Drive from Ballina along the Sligo section of the Wild Atlantic Way, passing through Enniscrone, Easky and Rosses Point, before driving further north to end up in Donegal town.

Day 2: Set off from Donegal town through the mountains towards Glenveigh National Park, then stop in Rathmullan on the way to Fanad.

Ballina is right on the edge of the Sligo/Mayo border and perched on the River Moy, which soon leads out to join the Atlantic. Stretch your legs first with a stroll along the riverside, or head out to the grounds of **Belleek Castle** nearby, where you can walk through the woods and grab a coffee in the café before heading off. Alternatively, pass by Jimmy's, a drive-thru coffee shop set up in a former petrol station – their doughnuts are fantastic, and each coffee comes with a little cube of chocolate brownie.

From there, follow the Wild Atlantic Way out along the **Sligo** coast, driving along the banks of the River Moy before you meet the wide, flat sands of **Enniscrone**. If you're a surfer, this is one of many spots in Sligo that will appeal, but it's also a great place for a seaweed bath. Kilcullens Seaweed Baths have been in operation since 1912 and is a good old-fashioned set up, with antique baths and retro wooden steaming pods.

Tracing the curve of the coastline, you'll soon be up in **Easky**, a charming village that's a good stop off point if you fancy a walk. Follow the path from the old stone bridge out along the sea, and in 10 minutes you'll get to the derelict tower of **Roslee Castle**, which you can enter. Further along the coast, **Poll Gorm** is a natural saltwater

Belleek Castle.

pool that disappears when the tide is high, and is a beautiful spot for a dip when the tides recede. You can always drive out there, if you'd prefer.

Continue on the Wild Atlantic Way, passing the rugged coast by **Aughris Head** (stopping at the thatched Beach Bar for a lunch of seafood chowder if you're peckish) until you reach Ballisadare. From there, you can carry on the Wild Atlantic Way and drive via Strandhill (page 22), or head straight to Sligo.

On the other side of town, **Rosses Point** is a brief coastal detour that'll take you to one of the prettiest towns in Sligo. If you fancy a pit stop, head for lunch in the Driftwood or Austie's, both known for their seafood, after a walk on the sandy beach. And if you're a sauna fan, the Hot Box sauna right on the edge of the sea is a perfect spot for a mid-drive sweat session – there are two saunas overlooking the water, a plunge pool and

steps down to the swimming point where you can cool off.

When you're back in the car, head up along the coastline with the distinctive peak of **Benbulben** to your right, and turn left at Cliffoney to see **Mullaghmore**. A mecca for big wave surfers, this curve of land is a beautiful spot on the coast – stop at Bishop's Pool, a natural swimming pool just to the side of the road.

Further north, you'll drive the teeny stretch of Leitrim's coastline – at 4km, it's the shortest in Ireland. There's now a brief walkway that takes you out to the sea, so you can see Leitrim's tiny beach.

Soon after, you're in **Donegal** and the town of **Bundoran**, which has undergone something of a resurgence in recent years – there are excellent cafés, a pristine beach and a pretty walkway along the shore. If you have some time, stroll the Rougey Cliff Walk to the Fairy Bridges, and watch people jump from the rocks into the sea.

Aughris Head.

Bundoran.

At the other side of Ballyshannon, you can choose to drive via the Wild Atlantic Way or simply stick on the N15 up to **Donegal Town**, where you'll stay for the evening – Lough Eske Castle and Harvey's Point are both great options.

Day 2 – Donegal to Fanad

You can opt to drive the Wild Atlantic Way up the Donegal coastline (page 68) but the inland scenery has just as much to offer. For the first stretch, you'll be weaving through the countryside, passing the shores of **Lough Eske** and sticking to the N15 as it goes through Ballybofey. But the further north you go, past the exits to Letterkenny, the better the backdrop gets, winding alongside heather-dappled mountains and tree-lined lakes – the road passes right by the beautiful Loughs Akkibon and Gartan. Before long you're skirting the edge of **Glenveigh National Park**, a place worthy of a few hours out of the car.

From the main car park, you can either get the shuttle bus up to **Glenveigh Castle** or walk the Lakeside Trail, a 3.5km pathway that runs from the visitor centre to the castle and gardens. Either way, it's a gorgeous route, the path running alongside Lough Beagh with benches dotted along the way where you can stop and drink in the view.

You can take a self-guided tour of the castle, which is a must for any history buffs, or indeed any cinema fans – Clark Gable, Marilyn Monroe and Greta Garbo have all stayed in the castle, and you can have a snoop around the parlours and drawing rooms where they would have gathered around the fire or the baby grand piano. There's even an outdoor swimming pool on the lakeshore, which would have had quite the party scene back in its heyday.

There are also elaborate gardens you can walk around, some of which date back to the 1880s, with ancient apple trees, glasshouses and an orangery, with beautiful views back to the battlements and tower of the castle. You can also do one of the walking loops that snakes through the woodland and the gardens, or up the mountain for a breathtaking view of the lake and the castle beneath.

Once you've worn yourself out, head back to the car and find the R255 to head east, passing by the 'Sword in the Stone' in the river. Cut across the middle of Donegal and you'll reach **Ramelton**, a pretty riverside village where you can stop for a bite to eat or a wander around the waterside.

The road then takes you up along the shores of **Lough Swilly**, going right on the water's edge until you meet **Rathmullan**. There are plenty of great places to grab a bite to eat – try the

Beachcomber Bar for fish and chips or a chowder, sitting outside if you can for great views of the water. Or head up to Rathmullan House, where there's a wood-fired pizza place set up in the garden in the summer months. Afterwards, take a walk on the sandy beach, dipping your toes in the calm water if the weather is playing ball.

From Rathmullan, it's around a 40-minute drive up to the northernmost tip of the peninsula, **Fanad Head**. The road meanders past Portsalon and Kerrykeel, with gorgeous views of the water and the mountains, before reaching **Fanad Lighthouse**, where you can park up and explore. The lighthouse itself is open for guided tours and gives a great insight into the historic life of a lighthouse keeper, starting in what was the living room with stories of

River in Ramelton.

Lough Swilly.

shipwrecks and treasure hunts, leading up to the top of the tower, a retro, turquoise blue space with, obviously, great views of the craggy coastline.

There are binoculars in the tower so you can keep an eye out for marine life, but it's also worth having a stroll around the headland before you go, to watch the wilds of the Atlantic smashing against the rocky outcrops, or to see the herd of straggly Highland cows who graze up the road. It's a particularly stunning sight at sunset, which you can breathe in if you book a night in one of the lighthouse keepers' cottages. Alternatively, drive back down the same road to check into the cosy Rathmullan House, which has a secret path right to the beach.

Fanad Lighthouse.

CONNACHT – Trip 5: 1 day
Leitrim and Roscommon

Sometimes, you don't want a big, multi-day road trip, but a shorter scoot around the countryside that you can comfortably get done within a day (or less, if you'd rather). This loop around the lesser-visited corners of Leitrim and Roscommon offers just that – you'll take in lake views, ancient forests and historic points of interest, on a manageable drive through picturesque countryside. In this part of the country, slow travel is all the rage. And while it makes for a great road trip, you can also extend the trip to see the countryside at a different pace, whether that's on a river cruiser boating up the Shannon, or on a leisurely cycle on the Blueway.

Need to Know

Duration: 1 day

Distance: 97km/60 miles

When to go: Midweek, to avoid any traffic

Start at: Carrick-on-Shannon

Finish at: Carrick-on-Shannon

The route

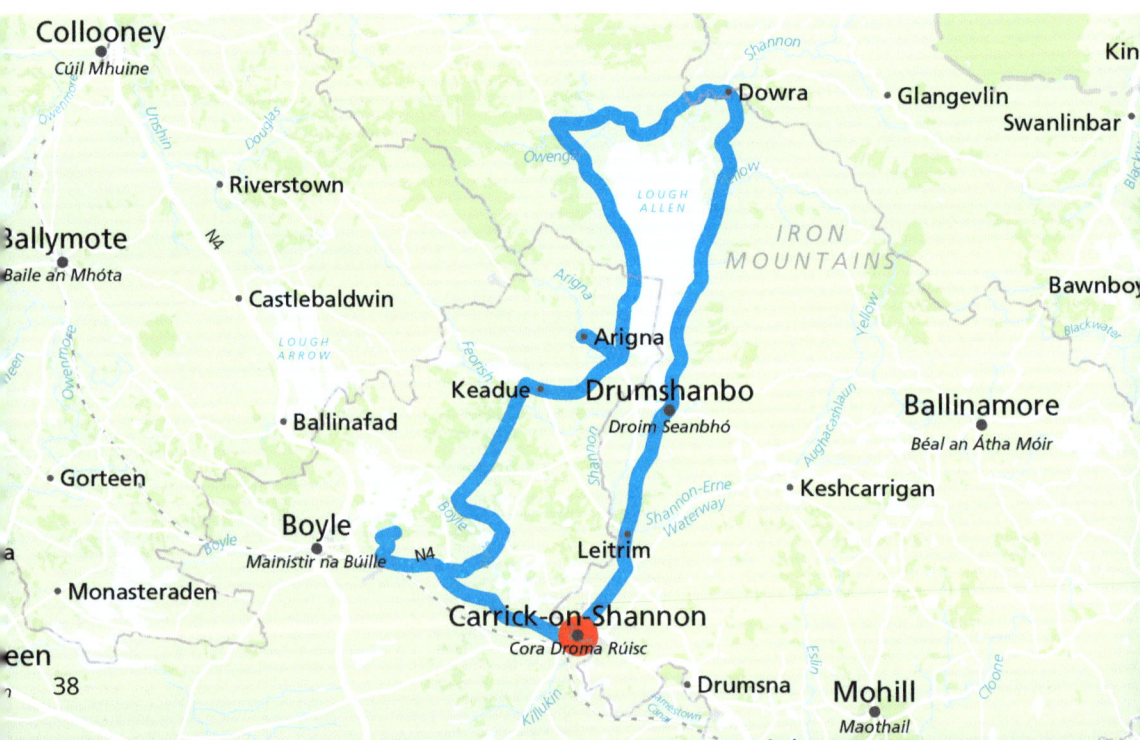

38

Quick view

Day 1: Head out of Carrick-on-Shannon towards Lough Key, where you can take a walk through the forest park. Then head to Arigna to tour the mining experience before driving around Lough Allen, stopping in Drumshanbo to see Acres Lake on the way back to Carrick.

Carrick-on-Shannon is a lovely town to potter around – start off on the riverside trail that follows the path of the Shannon, by community gardens and free library stands where you can pick up a book to read on a nearby bench. On Thursday mornings, there's a farmers market in the Market Yard, so you can pick up local delicacies and breads for a picnic. Just over the road, you'll find **Costello Chapel**, the second smallest church in the world. Peek through the glass floor and you can see the coffins of Edward and Josephine Costello – he built the church for his wife.

Around the corner, The Dock is an arts centre that regularly holds exhibitions and events, and it's also host to the Leitrim Design House where you can find excellent locally made artworks and crafts.

Start your road trip by heading out of the town on the N4, turning right before Boyle to visit **Lough Key Forest Park**. They offer a multitude of different activities here, many of which are focused on family fun like Zipit high wires or teamwork challenges. But it's also set on the shores of a beautiful lake, with several walking trails weaving through the historic estate, past old stone

McDermotts Castle on an island in Lough Key.

Lough Allen.

bridges, fairy villages and along the edge of the water. The 3.5km Drumman's Island Trail crosses one bridge over to an island, where you can also see the smaller lake isles dotted around, including the one nearby that's home to the remains of McDermott Castle.

Back on the road, you'll rejoin the N4 briefly before turning towards Cootehall, passing over the Boyle river where plenty of cruising boats pass through or park up in the marina. From there, the road loosely follows the river before you head over the rolling green countryside towards **Keadue**, where you'll follow the R285 to **Arigna**. Ireland's last working coal mine was right here in Roscommon, and at the **Arigna Mining Experience** you can go underground with guides who were miners themselves.

With a hard hat on, you'll head inside the mine to see and feel exactly how hard the life of a miner was, while learning about the history of the industry and the heritage of the Arigna Valley.

Back above ground, join the R280 for a scenic drive around **Lough Allen**, with the Corry Mountain Bog on one side and the water on the other. Stop off at **Spencer Harbour** if you've brought a picnic with you – this area is sheltered, with stunning views of the water.

When you reach **Drumkeeran**, turn right on the R200 to weave around the northern shore of the lake, crossing briefly into Cavan before heading down the R207 towards **Drumshanbo** on the other side of Lough Allen.

In recent years, one local brand has put Drumshanbo on the map, and that's

Gunpowder gin. Made just outside the village, this bottle is found in the best bars all over the world, and you can take a tour of **The Shed Distillery** to find out exactly how it's made. Non-drivers can taste a sample cocktail at the end, or you can pick up a bottle in the gift shop, where they sell special editions and collector's items you can only buy here.

On the other side of the village, **Acres Lake** is also drawing attention thanks to its floating boardwalk, which allows you to walk over the top of the water and swaying reeds to meet the **Shannon Blueway**, a path that follows the trail of the river. You can walk (or cycle) all the way to **Battlebridge**, which is about 6.5km in total, on a serene route that showcases the best of Leitrim countryside. Or you can take a stroll for as long as you please, before turning back to the car.

The drive back to Carrick-on-Shannon goes through **Leitrim** village, another popular spot for river cruisers who park up at the marina, before you're back in the town where you began.

Leitrim village.

MUNSTER – Trip 6: 1 day
Ring of Kerry

Before the Wild Atlantic Way swept in and stole the spotlight, the Ring of Kerry held the title of Ireland's most famous road trip. This 179km loop weaves around the Iveragh Peninsula, taking you through some of the most epic scenery that Kerry – and Ireland – has to offer. Be warned, though – this route can get very busy, particularly in the summer months, so it's best driven in the off-season. While the roads aren't as narrow as, say, the Slea Head Drive, it can be fairly tight in sections, and the coaches and tour buses can slow you down. They drive in an anti-clockwise direction, so your best bet is to head out clockwise, and stick to the shoulder seasons – the region is particularly beautiful in the autumn, but every bit as impressive in spring or even the bleak winter.

Need to Know

Duration: 1 day

Distance: 200km/124 miles

When to go: October, when the leaves are turning

Start at: Killarney

Finish at: Killarney

The route

Quick view

Day 1: Take the Ring of Kerry from Killarney down through the national park to Kenmare, then loop around the edge of the Iveragh Peninsula, adding the Skellig Ring, until you arrive back in Killarney.

Technically, you can start this loop at any point along the **Ring of Kerry**, but **Killarney** is as good a place as any to get cracking (Kenmare also makes a great starting point). There's also some flexibility in how long this drive will take you. The Ring of Kerry is essentially a looped road (mostly the N70) that encircles the peninsula, and you could technically drive the whole thing in less than four hours – if you didn't stop, that is. But if you want to get out to explore various sights along the way (and you should), it makes up a wonderful full day on the road. Our route is a little longer than the official Ring of Kerry loop, with a brief 20km detour to take in the Skellig Ring – however, you could always skip this and stick to the usual 179km route.

If you're starting off in Killarney, the first great stop is barely 10 minutes out of the town. Muckross House is a beautiful nineteenth-century building on the shores of **Muckross Lakes**, with elaborate gardens and great hiking trails. If you're staying in Killarney before your road trip, it might make sense to explore this the day before or after your drive, also calling in to see **Ross Castle** on Lough Leane – it's not technically on the Ring of Kerry, but is super close to Killarney and a particularly scenic spot.

Muckross Lakes.

Torc Waterfall .

Otherwise, the route is simple – all you need to do is follow the brown Ring of Kerry signs for the rest of the day. The road (initially the N71) takes you almost immediately into the stunning **Killarney National Park**, home to 10,000 hectares of breathtaking mountains, lakes, forests and waterfalls. Just beyond Muckross House is **Torc Waterfall** (which you can also hike to from the house itself), a five minute walk from the car park. The water cascades over mossy boulders in a deep green corner of the woodland, and is definitely worth a quick stroll. Bear in mind it can get busy, so set off from Killarney early if you want to explore it in peace.

Soon, the road will take you along the shores of **Muckross Lake**, running alongside a low stone wall as you make your way back into dense greenery. Next you'll meet **Owengarriff River**, a pretty stretch that leads into **Upper Lake Killarney**. The next must-see viewpoint

is **Ladies View**, an elevated spot that gives you an incredible lookout over the spherical mountains and lakes below. It gets its name from the visit Queen Victoria made with her ladies in waiting in 1861, and the views are almost as good at the next spot, **Looscaunagh Lough Viewpoint.**

Things get even more dramatic when you drive through **Moll's Gap**, where the landscape gets rockier and wilder, with great views of the **MacGillycuddy's Reeks**. If you fancy a coffee stop, there's an Avoca here, or you can carry on until you reach Kenmare. While the Ring of Kerry does pass through Kenmare, the route doesn't take you right into the centre. It's a pretty town though, so worth a wander if you can spare the time – you can always pick up a picnic lunch from Maison Gourmet, too.

From there, the route turns onto the N70, where you'll drive along Kenmare Bay, the water passing in and out of sight as you move through the dense woodland. As the road gets higher, the views get better, leading you past **Parknasilla** and into **Sneem**, where you can get a good lunch in the village pubs, if you're feeling peckish.

Afterwards, the road cuts into the mountains, meeting the water again soon after. If you fancy a brief detour, head to the beautiful sands of **Derrynane Beach**, about a five minute drive off the main road. The route flattens as you drive up past the coast by **Waterville**, where you'll find the famous golf links course.

At Kenneigh, you can either stick on the Ring of Kerry and head to the town of **Cahersiveen**, or turn left on the R567 to drive the extra 20km around the **Skellig Ring**. This loop takes you through Ballinskellig, where you can see the striking castle on the sands of the beach, past St Finian's Bay (where you'll find another great lunch spot, the Driftwood Surf Café) and Portmagee. If you want to see the Skellig Islands, you can get the

Castle ruins in Waterville.

boat from here, though bear in mind you'd want to stay the night locally, as fitting both this and the full Ring of Kerry into the schedule would be very tight indeed. Alternatively, you can drive over Valentia Bridge to The Skellig Experience Visitor Centre.

Otherwise, you'll drive back to meet the Ring of Kerry and continue up to

MacGillycuddy's Reeks.

Landscape near the village of Cahersiveen.

Cahersiveen and along the coast. The Mountain Stage Viewpoint is an excellent spot to get out of the car and look out over the ocean, before the route starts to cut inland after Killorglin to bring you back towards Killarney.

If you still have another bit of driving in you, turn off towards the **Gap of Dunloe**. Now, while you can technically drive this road, it's exceptionally narrow, winding and tricky if you meet any other traffic. A much better idea is to park at Kate Kearney's and walk the 1.3km down to the gap and back again – it's far prettier seen on foot, anyway.

When you're back behind the wheel, the road brings you right back into your starting point of Killarney, where your road trip is complete. Reward yourself with a spot of trad in a local pub, or a meal in one of the town's restaurants.

The Gap of Dunloe in an 1849 print from *Illustrated London News.*

Gap of Dunloe.

MUNSTER – Trip 7: 1 day
Burren Loop

In all likelihood, you've never driven over the surface of the moon (apologies to any astronauts who may be reading this book). But the good news is there's a viable alternative that's far closer to home. The Burren is an otherworldly tangle of vast limestone pavements and boulder-strewn fields, where things look distinctly grey upon first glance, but surprisingly colourful when you spot the tiny wildflowers growing between the crevices of the rock. The star of it all is the Burren National Park, and this route takes a detour to complete a gorgeous hike over the limestone there. But this region also has a cracking coastline and charming towns like Lisdoonvarna. It's also easy to add this onto the Clare stretch of the Wild Atlantic Way, if you want to combine two routes. Either way, here's how you can tick off all of the highlights in an easy day of driving.

Need to Know

Duration: 1 day

Distance: 81km/50 miles

When to go: April, when the wild orchids are in bloom

Start at: Ballyvaughan

Finish at: Ballyvaughan

The route

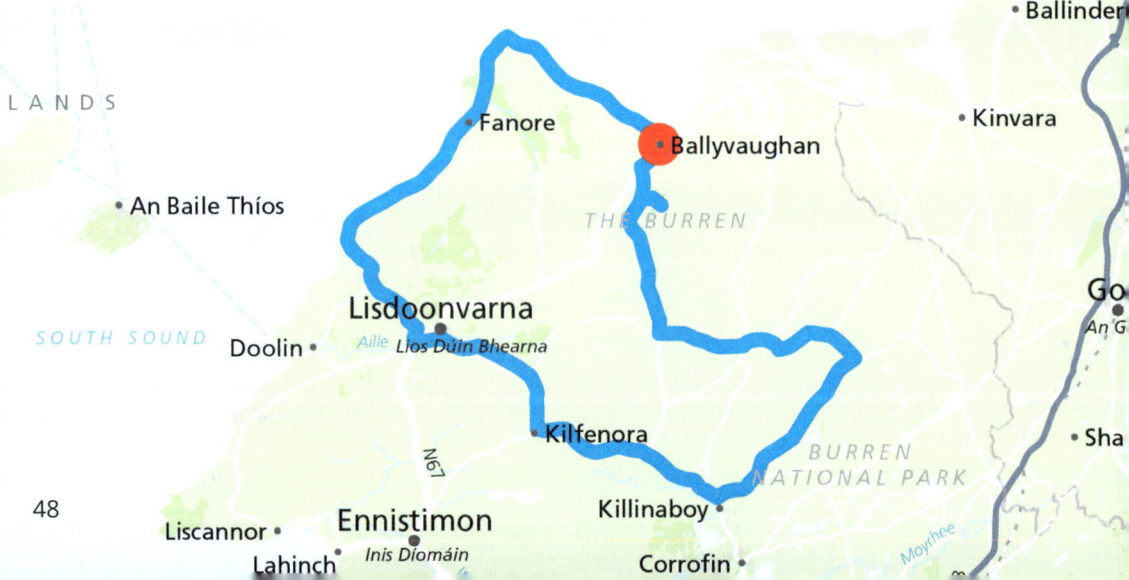

Quick view

Day 1: Drive from Ballyvaughan through the Burren, stopping for a hike at the national park before seeing the Clare coastline.

Corkscrew Hill.

You can drive this route in either direction, but it's marginally better to go clockwise, so that you're closest to the sea when you're driving up the Wild Atlantic Way. This loop starts in **Ballyvaughan**, a pretty fishing village where you can get breakfast in one of the cafés or tea rooms. If you want to stay somewhere more rural, Gregans Castle Hotel is a great shout – the nearby **Corkscrew Hill** is an interesting (read: nail-biting) short drive, too, zig zagging down to the coast.

But instead of taking that route all the way down the N67, this loop turns off to meet the R480, then driving the narrow Aillwee boreen through the countryside to reach the **Aillwee Burren Experience**. On a guided tour that leads you deep underneath Aillwee Mountain, you'll learn all about how this underground formation came to be, seeing the caverns and chasms along the way, as well as the remains of a European brown bear, estimated to be between 4,500 and 10,500 years old.

Back on the main road, you'll pass by several ring forts, and you can park up to explore **Cahermore Fort**

Ballyvaughan.

as well, if you desire. Otherwise, you'll carry on the R480, watching as the green fields start to get peppered with the limestone creeping up. You can get out at **Gleninsheen Megalithic Tomb** to see the ancient stone slabs, or at any of the accessible ringforts you'll also pass – this region is an archaeologist's paradise.

When you get to Leamaneh, turn left onto the R476 to head out into the **Burren National Park** proper. Unlike the other national parks, the visitor centre for this one is out in **Corofin**, where there's also a shuttle that will bring you into the hiking start points. But if you're

driving, you'll aim for the Gortlecka Crossroads, a rather nondescript point in the road but the trailhead for numerous excellent walks (there are trail maps and markers posted at this spot). Park at the roadside and pick your poison – there are shorter trails that take you out through the wildflowers (keep a close eye out for the wild orchids that are prolific in this region), or longer ones that take you up to the top of Mullaghmore mountain.

The best hike, however, is the **Lough Avalla Farm Loop**. This 7km will take about 2.5 hours to complete and is challenging in places (you'll definitely

Burren National Park.

Lough Avalla Farm Loop.

need good hiking shoes) but so worth it. Follow the purple arrows (some of which are progressively difficult to find on the limestone) and the loop will take you through pretty woodland, up and over the limestone pavement and past some incredible scenery, like the gentle slopes of Mullaghmore mountain, which looks a little like a deflated soufflé.

The loop finishes near Lough Avalla Farm House, and if it's open, it's a great spot to call into, run by the hiking farmers who own the land and make freshly brewed coffee, apple pie and chocolate cake for those walking through (be sure to bring cash).

Back in the car, you'll follow your tracks back towards Kilfenora, sticking on the R476 towards **Lisdoonvarna**. Along the way, you'll pass over the unique bogland of this area, sweeping past the old Spa Wells, which were an active

thermal bath house 200 years ago.

Stop into Lisdoonvarna to see the village famed for its matchmaking festival each September, then weave through the countryside on the narrow R477 until you reach the sea just beyond Ballyryan. From there, this stretch of

The Matchmaker Bar in the spa town of Lisdoonvarna.

Fanore Beach.

coastline is like no other, with sheets and slabs of gunmetal grey limestone to either side of the road, spreading all the way down to the ocean. You'll drive by the sea cliffs by *fulacht fia* ruins, and past any number of wedge tombs, promontory forts and megalithic ruins to your right.

Carry on up the mesmerising coastline, stopping at **Fanore Beach** to stretch your legs again, then keep heading north until you meet Black Head and its pretty lighthouse. Here, there are steps cutting through the rectangular slabs of limestone that head out to the water, and it's a unique sight to behold.

The R477 keeps looping around the coastline, passing by **Gleninagh Castle** on the shore, until you find yourself back in Ballyvaughan.

Fulacht fia at Drombeg Stone Circle.

Gleninagh Castle.

MUNSTER – Trip 8: 1 day
Slea Head Drive

Need to Know
Duration: 1 day
Distance: 42km/26 miles
When to go: April or May
Start at: Dingle
Finish at: Dingle

This relatively short road trip is so ridiculously scenic that you'll be glad of the numerous lookout spots peppered along the way – otherwise, the views are so distracting you'll find it hard to keep your eyes on the road. If you wanted to, you could drive the whole thing in one go in around an hour, but where's the fun in that? The best option is to allow a full day, allowing time to call into roadside food trucks for fresh crab rolls, properly explore the historic sites and spend at least an hour in the Great Blasket Centre. Here's how to make the most of one of Ireland's best road trips.

The route

Quick view

Day 1: Explore the looped Slea Head Drive from Dingle, calling at ancient forts, medieval bee hives and Dunquin Pier.

The route starts in **Dingle** itself, where you'll drive along the marina until you're just out of the town, then follow the brown Slea Head Drive signs for the rest of the day. Bear in mind that anyone driving the route for leisure purposes must go in a clockwise direction, so do stick to that rule to avoid causing a logjam later on.

The road starts out along the water, following the shore of the harbour until you reach **Ventry**, the first stopping point. If you're a football fan, you'll want to pay your respects at the statue of local footballer Páidí Ó Sé, which is set outside the pub of the same name.

As you head out of Ventry Harbour, you'll spot the first few ancient forts and *clocháns* (beehive huts) at the side of the road. Most of these sites are on farmer's fields, and entry is payable at the entrance – unless you're an avid history buff, you won't want to see them all.

Your best bet is to see **Dún Beag** fort, one of the first, which is set on a rugged and dramatic headland overlooking the wilds of the water below. This sixth-century promontory fort is somehow still intact, despite its precarious position, and your ticket also includes entry to the visitor centre at **Éalú**, just on the other side of the road (where you'll park). Once you've seen the video explaining the history of the fort, you can potter around the shop and get a coffee in the restaurant or,

Dingle.

even better, a freshly made crab roll with fries at Dobey's food truck, just next door – it's open seasonally, and it's well worth planning your trip around its opening hours. The crab comes from a friend of the owner's boat, and is served up in a buttery warm brioche bun with fries on the side.

If you have an interest in medieval history, the **Fahan Beehive Huts** make for a great stop and are just a little further up the road. On the green grassy slopes to the right of the road, there are 18 stone huts built by monks, all overlooking the sea below.

Soon after this stop, there's a hairpin

Fahan Beehive Huts.

turn to the left, with a shallow stream running over the road itself. Be sure to drive slowly on the approach, keeping an eye out for any cyclists or local traffic coming the other way – while leisure drivers must move in a clockwise direction, those who live on the road can drive against this traffic. If you do meet any other vehicles, make use of the laybys along the road that are designed for you to pull in and let someone pass.

As you pass over the stream and follow the road around the edge of the headland, you'll be met with views that just get better and better the further you drive. All of Dingle Bay is spread out before you, with the distinctive triangular peaks of the Skellig Islands in the distance, if you're lucky. The narrow road snakes around the curve of the coastline, with the deep green fields on your right and the expanse of ocean to your left, with jagged cliffs leading down to the water.

Pull in at **Coumeenoole Beach**, where you can park up (be warned, it does get congested on busy days) and walk down the slaloming path down to the sand, with high cliffs rising behind the shore

Dingle Bay.

Dunquin Pier.

and crystal clear sea. It's not a swimming beach, but it's a beautiful place to hop out and snap a picture.

There's one brief detour off the official Slea Head Drive that's a non-negotiable pit stop. **Dunquin Pier** is one of the ferry ports over to the Blasket Islands, but it's the unique zig zag shape of the road leading down to it that draws all the crowds. Follow the sign down to the pier and park up, before walking up above the road to get the best view. From the top, you can see the narrow path sharply criss-crossing back and forth down the steep, triangular hill, with smaller rocky isles to either side.

But don't, whatever you do, find a way

to drive down the walkway itself – one man did so in 2016 and he had to be rescued from his car by police.

There are usually a few coffee trucks parked up if you need a pick-me-up, but otherwise follow your tracks back up to the Slea Head Drive proper, passing Kruger's Bar, the most westerly pub in Ireland. About a kilometre later, turn at the sign for **The Blasket Centre**, the OPW-run space where you can learn all about life on the Blasket Islands, which are visible just over the water. After walking through the exhibits, head out to the viewing platform on the edge of the shore, where you get a fantastic view of Great Blasket. Bear in mind that entrance is free on the first Wednesday of every month (as is the case with plenty of OPW sites), if that coincides with your travels.

As the Slea Head Drive continues up and around the headland, you'll get more stunning views of the water, but it's worth pulling in at the stop for **Clogher Head**, where you can get out to see the curved white sand beach just over the bay.

After you pass through the village of **Ballyferriter**, the route moves inland, heading up and over the rolling hills of the peninsula. If you want to take a brief detour, you can turn off to the **Gallarus Oratory**, an ancient structure that dates

back to between the seventh and ninth centuries. Thought to be a place of reflection and safety for early Christian monks, it remains in remarkably good condition and forms a striking sight with Mount Bandon rising behind.

Once you're back on the road, you'll zoom through pristine countryside on a calm, straight road, until you reach the road back to Dingle.

There's plenty to keep you occupied for an evening, with numerous seafood restaurants, pubs and bars along the harbour's edge. Call into **The Fish Box** for top notch fish and chips, with the daily catch hauled in from local waters and

The dramatic Slea Head Drive coastal road.

Gallarus Oratory.

fried in a golden, perfectly crisp batter. If you can't get a table, or it's sunny out, head down to their food truck by the water for a dinner al fresco. **Out of the Blue** is a great shout if you're looking for elevated seafood – they serve whatever has been hauled in from the fishing boats that day.

Afterwards, there are any number of pubs hosting trad sessions, with music every night of the week, where you can wrap up the day with a pint and a session. Given there are over 50 pubs in Dingle, it's a safe bet that you can follow your nose (and the strains of a fiddle) and happen upon a good bit of music.

Traditional pub in Dingle town.

MUNSTER – Trip 9: 2 days
Beara Peninsula and Sheep's Head

Though it's just the next headland down from the Ring of Kerry, the Beara Peninsula gets a fraction of the traffic. But that doesn't mean it's any less striking – just that you're less likely to get stuck behind a coach as it navigates those narrow roads. A drive around this dramatically craggy, rough and ready stretch of land is nothing short of magical, and the very best that the West Cork landscape has to offer. The road meanders along the rock-lined shore, passing over ancient bridges and waterfalls as well as the pretty villages dotted around the peninsula. Adding another day to experience the (even wilder) Sheeps Head makes for a great two day road trip.

Need to Know

Duration: 2 days

Distance: 254 km/158 miles

When to go: May or early June, when attractions open for the season

Start at: Glengariff

Finish at: Ballydehob

You can take your time, stopping off at various sights along the way – taking the cable car to Dursey Island, or heading off on a detour to drive the Healy Pass – or you can spend your time behind the wheel, soaking in all the beauty from the car. But it's best to take a solid two days to really experience all that this corner of the country has to offer.

The route

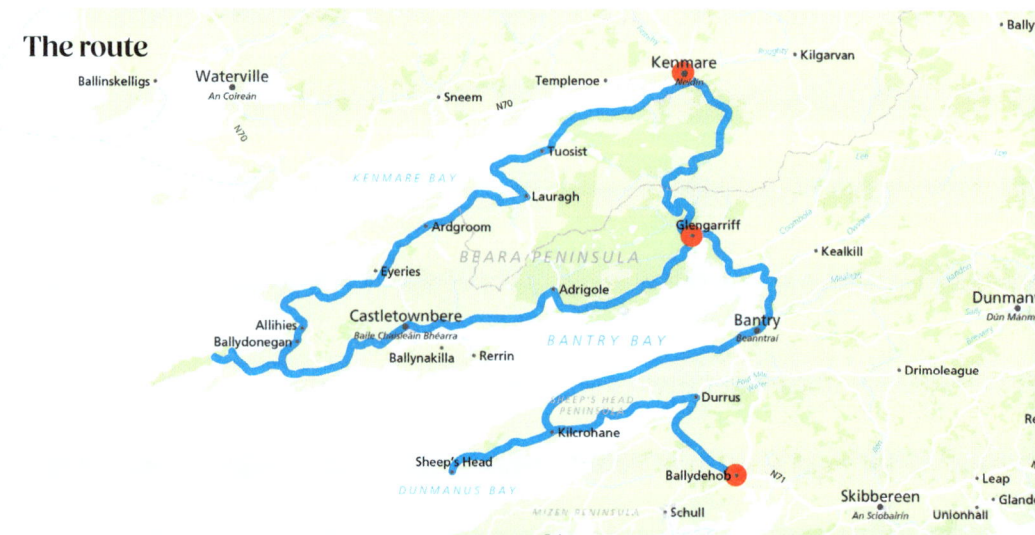

Quick view

Day 1: Depart Glengariff and drive all the way around the Beara Peninsula, stopping to take the cable car to Dursey Island and driving the Healy Pass, before finishing in Kenmare

Day 2: Drive the Caha pass from Kenmare down to Glengariff and Bantry, driving the Sheeps Head peninsula until you reach Ballydehob

Day 1 – Glengarriff to Kenmare

Start off the day at the bottom of the peninsula, in the pretty village of **Glengariff**. Sandwiched between the mountains and the sea, it's a lovely spot to explore for a day or so, if you can spare it before the road trip begins – you can take a walk down to the waters of **Bantry Bay** to see the ridiculously scenic Blue Pool or sit for a while at Deirdre's Lookout.

If you're a keen gardener, take the 15-minute ferry from Glengariff over to **Garinish Island**, a horticulturists' dream. From the shore, the island looks dense with greenery, but when you get into the interior you'll find a wealth of rare and beautiful flowers and plants – visit in the spring, and you'll get to see the azaleas and rhododendrons in full bloom. An added bonus? You might just spot the resident seals on the ferry journey. The ferries run from March to October.

When you're ready to get behind the wheel, head out on the southern stretch of the peninsula, following the

Bantry Bay.

R572 – officially the **Ring of Beara**. As the road takes you higher, the views of the rolling mountains get better and better, with rocky fields and bulbous slopes that undulate along the horizon. There's a scenic stop off point at **Whiddy Island View,** if you want to briefly stretch your legs, before the road continues through bogland and onto the village of **Adrigole**. This is a good spot for watersports, if you want to kayak with the seals or head out for a sail, but otherwise you have a choice as to your next destination.

You can continue on the Ring of Beara, or you can take a detour to drive the **Healy Pass**. Now, it would be a shame to come all this way and not see the famous road, but be warned that it is quite narrow and winding, so it's better suited to more confident drivers.

If that's you, turn off in Adrigole at the R574, following the brown signs for the Healy Pass. Surrounded by

Lauragh.

deep green fields, this single lane road snakes throughout the landscape like a scarf blowing in the wind, meandering alongside giant boulders and fields dotted with stone. There are a couple of viewing stops along the way (though some are

Healy Pass.

very small, with space for just one car), so your best bet is to pull in whenever you can spot a space (but never stop on the road if there's no layby).

If you want to, you can drive the whole 14km up to **Lauragh** in Kerry, then turn back to drive it all again to continue from Adrigole on the Ring of Beara. Alternatively, you could drive as far as the **Glanmore Lake** viewpoint and turn around (very carefully) at the small layby at the roadside – though this probably isn't an option on busy days.

Whatever you decide on, when you're back on the Ring of Beara you'll continue through the countryside, with occasional glimpses of the water to your left, until you reach **Castletownbere**. This is a great spot to stop off and have a little stroll, maybe stopping for lunch in one of the seafood restaurants along the water.

If you want to take another detour, and can spare a few hours in your itinerary, this is also the point where ferries depart over to **Bere Island**, and they go fairly regularly in the summer months.

Otherwise, crack on along the main route, where the road elevates before bringing you back down to the water's edge. Now, the next detour is one that's

Castletownbere.

Bere Island.

practically mandatory. Leave the main road to briefly join the L8905, following the signs to **Garinish**. The beach there is beautiful – as is the 5km hiking trail the Garinish Loop – but it's not your final destination. You're aiming for the end of the road and the **Dursey Island Cable Car**, the only one of its kind in Ireland and the only cable car in Europe that goes over open ocean. The ten minute crossing whisks you over to the island, with incredible views along the way. When you're there, you can amble around the walking trails and keep an eye out for interesting bird life, before getting the cable car back to the mainland. It runs all year, too.

Go back the way you came until you meet the Ring of Beara again, driving through the village of **Allihies**, once a hub of copper mining. In fact, the manmade beach nearby at Ballydonegan is made entirely of crushed quartz, not sand, which was a byproduct of the copper mining process. It's worth a closer look for the novelty factor alone, and the nearby **Allihies Copper Mine Museum** is a good spot if you want to learn more.

Back on the road, you'll pass by scenic Wild Atlantic Way markers like the Discovery Point at **Dooneen,** then carry along the narrow road as it clings to the edge of the peninsula, snaking around the coastline and bringing you increasingly beautiful views of the water.

Dursey Island Cable Car.

History or heritage buffs will want to stop briefly at the **Ballycrovane Ogham Stone**, just off the main loop, carved with the ancient ogham alphabet between 300 and 600 AD. In fact, this road goes past several ancient stone circles as well, if that's your style. Soon, you'll be in Lauragh (the Kerry side of the Healy Pass) before the coastal road takes you up and around the northern edge of the peninsula, passing **Kilmackillogue** on the way.

As you drive along, the waters of **Kenmare Bay** on your left and the rolling green hills of the Iveragh Peninsula rising up just beyond, you'll finish up the last section of the Beara Peninsula before crossing Our Lady's Bridge and heading straight into **Kenmare**, where you'll have more than earned a delicious meal in one of the town's many excellent restaurants. The pubs aren't bad, either ...

Day 2 – Kenmare to Ballydehob

Kenmare is a pretty market town, so start with a wander around to pick up a coffee, or perhaps a picnic for the road. If you happen to be there on a Wednesday, you're in luck – their weekly market falls on this day, and is a great spot to pick up artisan bread, homemade cakes and local fruit. Be sure to pop into Lorge Chocolatier too, for some chocolate and almond brittle or chilli-spiked truffles to enjoy over the course of the day.

Then it's time to hit the road, so head back over Our Lady's Bridge and follow the N71 all the way down towards **Glengariff** (incidentally, the road takes you right past the door of the Lorge Chocolatier factory, if you've already finished those truffles). You'll drive over the Releagh Bridge, and the traditional cottage experience at Molly Gallivans Visitor Centre, before driving through the rock tunnel at the **Caha Pass**, right on the border of Kerry and Cork.

The road takes you through the mountains, winding through the slopes until you end up back in Glengariff. Just before the village, you'll pass by

Kenmare Bay.

Caha Pass.

Glengariff Nature Reserve, which is a lovely place for a stroll – and if you didn't have time to go to Garinish Island yesterday, you can hop over today, as there's less driving to be done.

Otherwise, follow the N71 (now the Wild Atlantic Way) and continue to **Bantry**, which is a good place to stop for a bite to eat or a coffee. Afterwards, drive just outside the town to **Bantry House** – the estate is open from April to October and is hugely impressive, the grand eighteenth-century house overlooking the tiered Italian gardens and Bantry Bay beyond. It's worth taking a guided or self-guided tour of the house – owned and lived in by the descendants of the Earls of Bantry – to see the incredible artwork inside. Do take some time to stroll the gardens too, and stop into the tearooms before you leave.

Just after Abbey Beach, take a right to follow the signs for Goats Path, where you'll soon meet the **Sheeps Head Peninsula**. This isn't as popular a driving route, so you'll find you may have the roads to yourself (bar the odd

hiker crossing over). The road is super narrow, however – more of a boreen in some places – but a gorgeous route for a confident driver, with thickets of fern and greenery to either side and the waters of Bantry Bay beyond.

Take your time driving, making your way down to the tip of the headland, pulling over when you spy a good viewpoint – **Fionn Mac Cumhaill's Seat** is a good one, the stone bench inscribed with the words 'water and ground in

Bantry House.

Disused railway viaduct in Ballydehob.

their extremity', from a poem by Seamus Heaney.

While the really keen hikers take on the full 88km long walking trail that weaves around the shore, there are plenty of options for people who want to just walk a shorter loop. The best of these options are right at the tip of the headland, so take a right at Kilcrohane to drive out as far as the road stretches, passing little lakes along the way, until you reach Sheep's Head Walk – Tooreen Turning Point, where you can park up and pick up a cuppa in Bernie's Cupán Tae, if it's open.

Then get out of the car and walk out to the **Sheep's Head Lighthouse**, passing

Lough Akeen and following the well-trodden footpath out to the very tip of the headland. It's worth the effort – though the walk takes around two hours in total and can be steep and rough underfoot, the sight of the lighthouse clinging to the edge of the rocks is top notch.

When you're back in the car, follow your route back to Kilcrohane then drive along the southern edge of the peninsula, right along the water's edge, until you meet **Durrus** and the end of the headland. From there, turn right onto the R591 past **Blairs Cove**, then left on the (narrow) Mine Road until you reach **Ballydehob**, purely because it's a lovely place to spend the night.

Sheep's Head Lighthouse.

Wild Atlantic Way

When it comes to Irish road trips, the Wild Atlantic Way is the star of the show. Conceived in 2015 (though the roads themselves are far older), this 2,500km long route snakes all the way up Ireland's western shore, from the Cork fishing village of Kinsale to Donegal's Inishowen Peninsula. Along the way, you get to take in the best of this rugged, showstopping coastline, be it on tiny boreens that wind along empty stretches of sand, or on roads that hug the clifftops as waves batter the shore hundreds of feet below. Whenever you see a giant, rusty waymarker at the roadside, you know that's a sign to pull in and get out the car – these jagged 'Discovery Points' mark the most scenic spots along the route.

But the best part of the Wild Atlantic Way is how customisable it is. Sure, you could spend two weeks driving the whole thing in its entirety, seeing every inch of the route and turning it into the trip of a lifetime. Or you could simply drive one short section, dipping in and out wherever you please. It's also worth noting that the route isn't entirely linear – at some points, the road juts out into paths that take you to a particularly scenic spot before coming back to join the main stretch. Whether you want to see them all is entirely up to you – this is your road trip, after all.

Here, we've divided the Wild Atlantic Way into four sections, which you can drive separately or all in one long, glorious go.

Need to Know

Duration: 2 weeks

Distance: 2,500km/1,600 miles

When to go: September

Start at: Kinsale

Finish at: Malin Head

Quick view

Section 1: Drive from Kinsale out to Dingle, taking in the West Cork coastline and the iconic Beara and Iveragh Peninsulas.

Section 2: Set off from Dingle and see some more of the Kerry shore, before exploring Clare and heading into Galway.

Section 3: This section takes in the gorgeous Connemara coastline, before moving through the wilds of Mayo into Sligo.

Section 4: Starting from Sligo, this coastline gets more and more wild as you move up to Donegal and the finishing point at the Inishowen Peninsula.

Stage One – Kinsale to Dingle
Day 1 – Kinsale to Skibbereen

Technically, the Wild Atlantic Way begins on the R600 just outside **Kinsale,** but unless you want a photo of the (rather nondescript) sign announcing it, you're better off starting in Kinsale proper. Before you get in the car, take an hour or so to stroll along the **Scilly Walk** out to **Charles Fort.** This pathway clings to the edge of the shore, taking you past the boats bobbing on the harbour and alongside the lust-worthy houses on the water, until you reach the seventeenth-century star-shaped fort itself. The views out over the water are fantastic, and you can also take a guided tour and hear all about the fort's resident ghost.

If you have the time, a pit stop at The Spaniard Inn or the Bulman Bar is a must – these charming pubs are right on the Scilly Walk and do a roaring trade in local lobster when it's in season. And if you stay the night in Kinsale before you begin, there are any number of excellent restaurants in the town, most of which specialise in seafood, from shellfish platters in Fishy Fishy to the Michelin-starred Bastion.

The first stop along the Wild Atlantic Way is a good one. **The Old Head of Kinsale** is barely a 20-minute drive from the town, and while you can't access the very tip of the peninsula (that's the domain of the golf course) you do pass over the rolling green headland and get the clifftop views along the way.

Stop instead at the small **Lusitania Museum & Old Head Signal Tower** – there's a memorial statue outside, which frames the very spot where the ship was torpedoed just off the coast. The cliffs at

The route

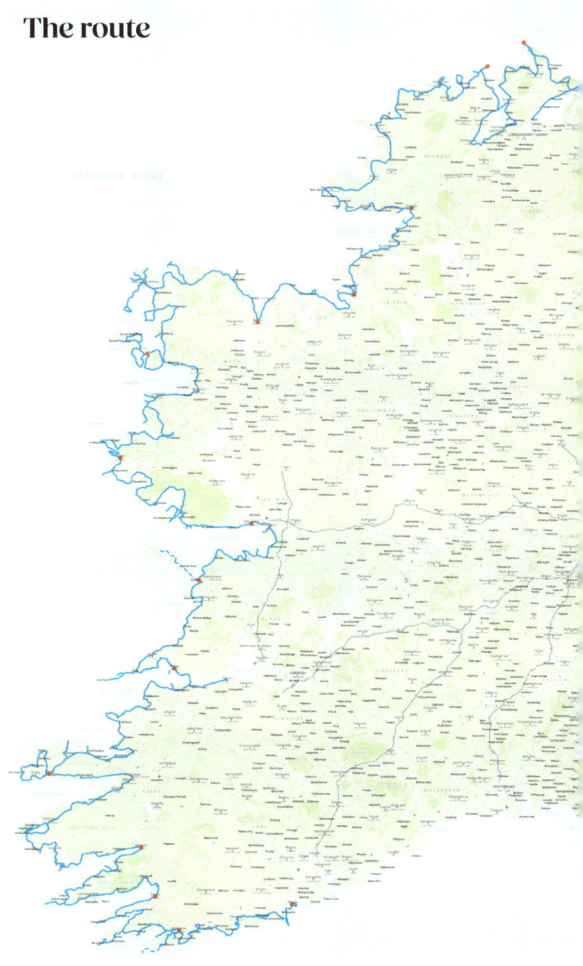

the Old Head are spectacular, the rocks jutting into the waves like fingers.

From there, the coastal road takes you past the wide, sandy beaches of **Garrettstown** and **Harbour View**, with the sea on your left as you approach Timoleague. If you fancy a detour, the Wild Atlantic Way then cuts back on itself to **Courtmacsharry**, but you can also stick on the westerly stretch inland towards **Clonakilty**. Just before the town, you'll rejoin the coastal road, taking in **Inchydoney, Rosscarbery** and **Glandore,** where you'll be a short hop from the pretty spot of **Leap,** where you can stop for lunch in Connolly's of Leap.

The road takes you up and over some ridiculously scenic viewpoints, from the pretty harbour of **Unionhall** to the curve of **Castlehaven Bay,** cutting down to **Toe Head** before winding back up to **Skibbereen,** which is the ideal spot to park up and call it a day. Be sure to call into one of the town's cosy pubs for a pint, if that's up your alley.

Day 2 – Skibbereen to Bantry

From Skibbereen, the Wild Atlantic Way technically splinters into three different offshoots, which means you can choose to drive all three, or pick the one that suits you best. One takes you down to **Lough Hyne,** a sea lough known for its bioluminescence (night kayaking there in the summer is an otherworldly experience), then back up before rejoining the road to **Baltimore** (with a quick detour to **Inishbeg).**

In truth, you could spend the entire day in this neck of the woods, taking the ferry out to **Cape Clear,** a car-free Gaeltacht island with beautiful hiking, before coming back to walk to the **Baltimore Beacon** and have dinner in the Michelin-starred Dede.

Otherwise, it's back on the road that leads you to the highlights of West Cork,

A panoramic landscape view of Inchydoney Beach.

Baltimore Beacon is a white-painted stone beacon at the entrance to the harbour at Baltimore.

taking you first to the tip of **Cunnamore**, before weaving back to **Ballydehob** (another village that could easily warrant a day or two of your time). The road then takes you to **Schull** before curving down the bottom of the **Mizen Peninsula** to the most south-westerly point on the Irish mainland, **Mizen Head.** You can visit the **Mizen Head Signal Station**, but the most impressive part is simply crossing the bridge on foot, keeping an eye on the water for the native whales and dolphins.

Once you pass **Durrus,** the route takes you down the **Sheep's Head Peninsula,** also home to the 88km walking trail the Sheep's Head Way. Now, that's a fairly hefty multi-day trek, but you can also hike shorter sections if you want to stretch your legs. And if not, you'll still be able to take in the rugged beauty of the peninsula from behind the wheel (see more on page 60). When you head back up the northern edge of the headland, you'll end up in **Bantry,** where you'll stay for the night.

Day 3 – Bantry to Kenmare

This stage of the Wild Atlantic Way serves up one of the best days of driving you could ask for – the **Beara Peninsula.** This untamed wonder of coastline has its own chapter, so if you want to drive the Ring of Beara you can read more on page 62. Finish up in **Kenmare**, where you can make your base for the night.

Day 4 – Kenmare to Dingle

If the Wild Atlantic Way is Ireland's best-known road trip, then the **Ring of Kerry** comes in at a (very) close second. For years, this was the pinnacle of Irish driving routes, and it's still an absolute corker. This day on the Wild Atlantic Way takes in most of the route, weaving from Kenmare all around the edge of the **Iveragh Peninsula** until you reach **Killorglin.** For information on the full route information, turn to page 42.

Instead of turning back in to drive the **Gap of Dunloe** down to Kenmare, carry on the coast until you reach Dingle, driving on the south of the **Dingle Peninsula** past the beautiful **Inch beach** and up over the headland.

Stage 2 – Dingle to Galway
Day 1 – Dingle to Kilrush

You could easily spend a few days in **Dingle,** exploring the **Blasket Islands,** taking a boat trip around the base of the huge, jagged cliffs and checking out the trad music scene in the many pubs scattered around the village.

But when you're ready to hit the road, you'll be driving on one of the best independent road trip routes in the country. The **Slea Head Drive** is short, but it sure does pack a punch when it comes to breathtaking Irish scenery. Read about the route in full on page 54.

The Slea Head drive finishes back in Dingle, where you'll head out the other side of the town and cut across the peninsula on one of the most striking

Aerial panoramic landscape view of the Kerry Cliffs and Iveragh Peninsula in County Kerry.

Mountains and cliffs at the Conor Pass on the Ring of Kerry's Wild Atlantic Way.

routes you could ever ask for – the **Conor Pass.** This 12km road looks like it's leapt straight from a postcard, the winding route climbing steeply up the side of lush green mountains to give outstanding views over the Kerry countryside.

Like Slea Head, the road is narrow with a very sharp drop on the side, so be sure to drive slowly and carefully, pulling in at one of the designated stopping points if you need to let another car pass.

Once you're on the other side, you can take a pit stop at **Lough Adoon** before detouring up to Ballydavid, or driving the northern edge of the peninsula to **Castlegregory beach** and back towards **Tralee.**

Here, the road passes by **Fenit, Ballybunion** and the wilds of the northern Kerry coastline before you reach the border with Limerick. The Wild Atlantic Way reaches along this stretch of the Shannon Estuary towards **Foynes,** where you can visit the **Flying Boat Museum.** But to cross over to the next stretch of coast, the easiest option is to take the car ferry from **Tarbert** to **Killimer,** crossing the Shannon until you reach Clare.

From there, Kilrush is less than a 15-minute drive away.

Day 2 – Kilrush to Doolin

If you have the time, a boat trip out to **Scattery Island** is a pleasant way to spend a few hours. You might spot some of the rare Shannon dolphins on the 15-minute crossing, and when you're there you can take an OPW tour of the sixth-century monastery settlement, learn about the rare native birds who nest on the island, and walk around the peaceful isle to the old lighthouse.

Otherwise, it's on to the **Loop Head Drive,** a beautiful route that will take you along the top of bright green cliffs, past blowholes and to the lighthouse at the very tip of the headland. You can also stay the night at the lighthouse keeper's

Aerial photograph of the Cliffs of Moher.

cottage, if that takes your fancy. You'll pass by the **Kilkee Cliffs**, where you can get out and stroll along the clifftop path for a windswept break from the car.

Beyond **Kilkee,** the roads cuts ever so slightly inland to move up the Clare coastline, past **Doonbeg** and up to **Spanish Point,** where you can hop out at the memorial to those who died when two of the Armada ships wrecked offshore.

From there, the road takes you to Lahinch, over the pretty stone bridge that crosses the Inagh River as it reaches the sea, and through **Liscannor,** where you can take the turn to see the Discovery Point at **Clahane**. The next stop is one of the most famous coastal landmarks in Ireland – the **Cliffs of Moher.**

If you can time it right, sunset is the perfect time to see the cliffs in all their glory – depending on the time of year, this will mean the tour buses will be gone, and the crowds will have dispersed for the day. But even late afternoon will give you a bit of reprieve, and the light dimming over the cliffs will be at its finest.

Take a walk up to **O'Brien's Tower,** which gives you a great vantage point over the cliffs – you can also climb to the top, though you may have to wait in line. There are generally fewer people on the walk south, where you can stroll along the clifftop path for as long as it's deemed safe. If you're there in the early summer, borrow a pair of free binoculars from the visitor centre (where there's also an excellent immersive 4D presentation

Medieval O'Brien's tower at the Cliffs of Moher,

called The Ledge) to keep an eye out for puffins nesting almost immediately below.

When you're finished, the drive to **Doolin** only takes around 10 minutes, and there are plenty of trad sessions to keep you occupied before bed.

Day 3 – Doolin to Galway

They're not technically a stop on the Wild Atlantic Way, but if you're in this corner of the country then it would be a shame not to add on another day to see the **Aran Islands.** Ferries depart from Doolin to all three of the islands, so a day trip to whichever one takes your fancy is easy. **Inis Oírr** is the closest, so you could do a whistlestop tour in the morning, taking the first ferry and returning at lunchtime, renting bikes from the harbour to whizz around this charming island. Alternatively, you could take an hour-long boat trip from Doolin to the base of the Cliffs of Moher, to see this landmark from the water.

Back on the Wild Atlantic Way, the road skirts along the edge of the **Burren,** the limestone pavement giving the roadside a uniquely stark, otherworldly appearance (you can add on a day to drive the Burren

Spectacular landscape in the Burren.

Loop, on page 48). Pause at the **Flaggy Shore** to recite some Seamus Heaney, then continue along this gorgeous stretch of coast through **Kinvarra** and over the Galway border until you reach the city, where you'll stop for the night.

Stage 3 – Galway to Sligo
Day 1 – Galway to Clifden

From Galway, the Wild Atlantic Way follows the R336 past **Spiddal** and **Ballynahown Pier,** along the southern edge of **Connemara.** You also pass by the tiny Connemara Airport at Inverin, where you can catch an even tinier plane for a scenic crossing over to the Aran Islands, if you don't fancy the ferry option.

The route then passes down to **Carraroe,** leading you to the unique Coral Strand, before heading back up to cross the incredibly picturesque causeways to the stark beauty of **Lettermore,** birthplace of the famous Connemara ponies. You have to drive back to Costelloe to rejoin the road, which passes by the tiny scattering of islands on the way up to **Screebe.** From there, you'll skim the coastline as you pass by the quintessentially Connemara landscape, with gently curved mountains at the roadside and islands occasionally visible from the road.

The next key stop is **Roundstone,** which is a great spot to have lunch before getting back in the car and driving on to **Clifden,** your stop for the night. You can see more on this route on page 15, though a Wild Atlantic Way addition is a brief stop in **Bunowen Beach,** near the Connemara Smokehouse, where you can pick up artisanal smoked salmon.

Day 2 – Clifden to Achill

Your day starts with a treat, driving the beautiful **Sky Road** before moving along the coast towards **Letterfrack** and **Renvyle** – read our guide to this route on page 17. But instead of retracing your steps back to Letterfrack on the L1101, the Wild Atlantic Way heads out along the coast to the heavenly **Glassilaun Beach,** then skims the edge of **Lough Fee** until you reach **Killary Fjord.** You'll drive all the way around the water, past **Leenaun** and into Mayo and **Aasleagh Falls,** until you go through Delphi and

Sky Road, with a Wild Atlantic Way sign, near Clifden town in Connemara, County Galway.

Dawn over Clew Bay and Croagh Patrick mountain, from Old Head, County Mayo.

swap the Atlantic for some lakeshores for a short spell.

The mountain ranges grow all the more imposing as you pass **Mweelrea** and the **Doolough Valley,** where curved golden peaks circle the lakes. The road sweeps back down towards the **Lost Valley**, a desolate stretch of white sands, boulder-strewn fields and bulbous mountains. By way of **Carrownisky Beach**, you'll find **Roonagh,** perhaps best known as the ferry port between the mainland and Clare Island. The homeland of Grace O'Malley (AKA the Pirate Queen), this island is a fascinating place to explore, though you'd need to do so on foot as it's a passenger ferry only.

Back on the Wild Atlantic Way, the road meanders along the Mayo coastline to **Louisburgh**, with fantastic views of **Clew Bay** and its 365 islands (one for every day of the year, as locals will always remind you). The route takes you right into **Westport**, an endearing town with a fantastic food and music scene, so stop here for the night or drive on towards **Mulranny.**

Day 3 – Achill to Ballina

Achill deserves a full day of dedicated exploring, so head to page 24 to check out the route. That drive ends back in Mulranny, and if you wanted proof that the Wild Atlantic way isn't one simple road, this day behind the wheel will prove it. But what this route lacks in linear mapping, it more than makes up for in untamed beauty. This corner of Mayo, perhaps because it's a little off the beaten track, doesn't get nearly as much attention as it deserves. Get an early start, so you can see as much as possible, and head to North Mayo.

The initial stretch moves north on the N59, past the **Wild Nephin National Park** until you reach **Bangor-Erris,** before heading west to loop around **Doohoma Head.** On the way up to **Erris Head,** you'll pass the sandy expanse of **Doolough Beach** and **Claggan Bay,** before driving over the spit of land to **Belmullet** and the peninsula proper.

Here, the road splinters into four different options, the first taking you south to **Blacksod,** along a stark and beautiful expanse stretching down to the lighthouse, where you can hop out for a quick walk. This is also where the boats depart for **Inishkea Island,** which is well worth the excursion if you have a day spare – these get a fraction of the footfall that others do, but have blindingly white sand beaches, abandoned villages and a seal colony.

Move back up north, passing **Elly Bay Beach,** and your next Discovery Point is **Ceann an Eanaigh,** where you'll find the oldest rocks on the Irish mainland. The next is just a 15-minute drive away at **Dún na mBó,** a natural blow hole that's a showstopper when the winds are wild (as they often are). A sculpture frames the natural landmark, turning it into a geological piece of art, and the crashing waves that power through the rock are mesmerising.

The spirit of windswept wonder continues at the next stop, the **Erris Head Loop Walk.** If you have a couple of hours to spare, the full 5km loop is incredible, leading you over the lush grassy headland overlooking the sea cliffs

Erris Peninsula, Erris Head Loop Walk, Glenamoy, Belmullet, County Mayo.

Sunset over a tidal pool at Belmullet.

and the dramatic waves below. But you can also just walk a shorter stretch and return to the car whenever suits.

There is, however, another excellent hike at the next stop, **Carrowteige,** which takes you to **Benwee Head.** It is, however, much longer at around 13km, so you'll need to plan accordingly for a walk that'll take about 5 hours. If you'd rather, you can drive to **Rinroe Beach,** a minor detour for a spot not technically part of the Wild Atlantic Way, but a stonker of a bay all the same. If you did want to explore this area in more depth, you can stay the night in **Belmullet,** rather than **Ballina.**

The Dún Briste sea stack off the cliffs of Downpatrick Head in County Mayo.

But if you're pushing on, you'll reach one of the coolest spots in Mayo, **Downpatrick Head.** The road sneaks along the blustery northern shore, past **Céide Fields** (a good stop for any archaeology enthusiasts) until you turn for the Discovery Point, where you can park up and walk the short distance over the headland to see the **Dún Briste Sea Stack.** The ground bounces underfoot, the result of bogland roots creating springy domes of grass, and when you reach the edge you can see seabirds flitting between the cliffs and the impressive sea stack just offshore.

From there, you'll drive down into **Ballina,** where you'll almost certainly need a rest.

Day 4 – Ballina to Sligo

If you slept in Ballina instead of Belmullet, there's a simpler day of driving ahead, skimming the Mayo coastline briefly until you reach Sligo, passing by the beaches of **Enniscrone, Easky** and **Aughris** – turn to page 33 for details.

Stage 4 – Sligo to Donegal
Day 1 – Sligo to Donegal town

This coastline in the Northwest of the country is stunning, with dramatic sea cliffs, big waves and striking mountains along the way. The route from Ballina to **Donegal Town** on page 35 takes you mostly along the Wild Atlantic Way, missing only Rossnowlagh beach, so follow that road trip for day one.

Day 2 – Donegal to Fanad

There's an inland route from Donegal Town to Fanad on page 35, which takes you through the beautiful **Glenveigh National Park.** But the coastal route has a whole other beauty, starting on the beachy side of South Donegal. You'll drive through **Inver, Killybegs** and **Muckross,** passing the Secret Waterfall right on the coast, before the route cuts into the mountains to take you to **Sliabh Liag.**

Seal resting on a pier in Killybegs, County Donegal.

These sea cliffs are taller than the Cliffs of Moher and more remote in feel, reached via a short hike from the car park (or a shuttle bus). At the top, you can take in the sight from the viewpoints, or walk up the steep steps for a better view – they're particularly striking after a spell of heavy rain, when the cliff face is streaked with waterfalls.

Looping back to meet the R263, the route continues through the Donegal mountains, detouring to the Gaeltacht village of **Malin Beg** and the horseshoe beach **Silver Strand.** You'll head back across the rolling green hills to rejoin the N56, pausing first at the **Glengesh Viewing Point** for a fabulous vantage point of the mountains.

The roadside gets a little more untamed the further north you go, past Donegal Airport (frequently named the most scenic landing in the world) and up to the beach at **Cnoc Fola** (Bloody Foreland). But don't worry, it gets its name from the rusty colour the headland turns at sunset, or when the autumn colours are in full bloom.

The road snakes through the coastal countryside until you reach **Dunfanaghy,** an excellent spot to stop for a seafood lunch or to stay the night. Nearby, **Horn Head** isn't actually the northernmost point on the Wild Atlantic Way, but when you're standing right at the summit it sure does feel like it. The weather can change by the minute, but the views are spectacular, with rolling mountains thick with heather and gorse, and dramatic cliffs that look like they've been created with layers of stone slabs.

If you are staying in Dunfanaghy, it's also worth trekking to **Trá Mór**, a gorgeous beach accessible only on foot. The walk takes about 45 minutes from the town, but when you get to the sand, you'll likely have it all to yourself.

Otherwise, crack on the coastal road past **Marble Hill** (a great surf spot) to the next peninsula, looping around the headland from **Downings** and over to the next in line, crossing the Harry Blaney Bridge at **Mulroy.** The road carries on north, past **White Shore Beach** until you creep up the **Fanad Peninsula** to the lighthouse that gives it its name (see page 36).

Day 3 – Fanad to Malin Head

The tip of Donegal splits into peninsulas that jut into the Atlantic like fingers. The next one after Fanad is the **Inishowen Peninsula,** and the northernmost point on the Irish mainland, **Malin Head.** From Fanad, the Wild Atlantic Way hugs the shoreline as the sea meets Lough Swilly, curving down to the pretty towns of Rathmullan and Ramelton (see page 36).

When you reach **Letterkenny,** the road goes east up to the **Malin Peninsula,** first stopping near Inch Island, a must-see for any birdwatchers. Connected to the mainland by bridge, this island has a huge population of migratory birds like Whooper swans and rare geese, who return in the autumn. You can also explore the remains of the fifteenth-century **Inch Castle.**

Just beyond Buncrana, you'll drive through the scenic **Gap of Mamore** (see page 135) before finally reaching **Malin Head,** the very end of the Wild Atlantic Way.

Malin Head at sunset, Ballyhillin, County Donegal.

MUNSTER – Trip 11: 2 days
Tipperary Highlights

This corner of the country often comes up trumps in the 'top places to travel' lists – and when you drive around the Tipperary countryside, it's clear to see why. There's a gorgeous combination of rolling green fields, mountain drives and gnarled forests, with charming towns and villages along the way that are perfect for a pit stop. But there are also the historic sites that are peppered around the county, with ancient castles and one of Ireland's most famous landmarks, the Rock of Cashel, forever drawing the crowds. It's also a hotspot for excellent food and produce, with local favourites like Cashel Blue cheese, Inch House pudding and Galtee Honey all made within county lines. You can visit some of them in person, but either way, you'll find almost all on café and restaurant menus.

Need to Know

Duration: 2 days

Distance: 222km/138 miles

When to go: May, when more historic sites are open

Start at: Portumna

Finish at: Dungarvan

Then there's the real star of the show – Lough Derg. Right in the middle of Ireland's Hidden Heartlands, this giant lake marries the counties of Clare, Tipperary and Galway, with a long narrow shape that looks more like a river when you look at it on the map. Along its shores, you'll find pretty little villages that burst into life in the summer, their harbours filled with fishing boats and river cruisers, with people mooring up to pop into the pub for lunch. It's a prime spot for fishing, but you'll also find a wealth of activities available on the water, from kayaking trips and stand up paddle boarding to sailing and high speed RIB tours.

While you could easily tick off this road trip in two days, you could also allow three if you wanted to spend more time in places like Limerick or Cashel along the way.

Quick view

Day 1: Head from Portumna in County Galway along the shores of Lough Derg until you end up in Limerick for the night.

Day 2: From Limerick, drive through the Tipperary countryside, stopping in Cashel, before seeing Cahir and driving the Vee to reach Lismore, then winding up in Dungarvan.

Day 1 – Portumna to Limerick

This trip kicks off in **Portumna**, gateway to the River Shannon and Lough Derg. It's worth spending a morning or afternoon here, particularly if you're an avid walker – the nearby **Portumna Forest Park** has an old abbey and castle on its 450 hectares, as well as hiking trails that weave through the woodland. There's also a new bird hide, where you can keep watch to try and sneak a peek at the park's newest visitor, a white-tailed sea eagle who has hatched chicks.

When you're ready to hit the road, head out on the N65 before curving around the top of the lake to your first stop, **Terryglass**. This pretty village is a hub for visiting boats and cruisers during the summer months, but is every bit as charming in the off-season – park up in the village and stroll the few minutes down to the harbour to snoop at the boats. If you're looking for lunch or a coffee stop, there are a couple of cosy gastropubs where you can grab a bite.

Otherwise, get on the R493 and continue through the Tipperary countryside, catching occasional views of the lake as you drive through woodland and alongside

The route

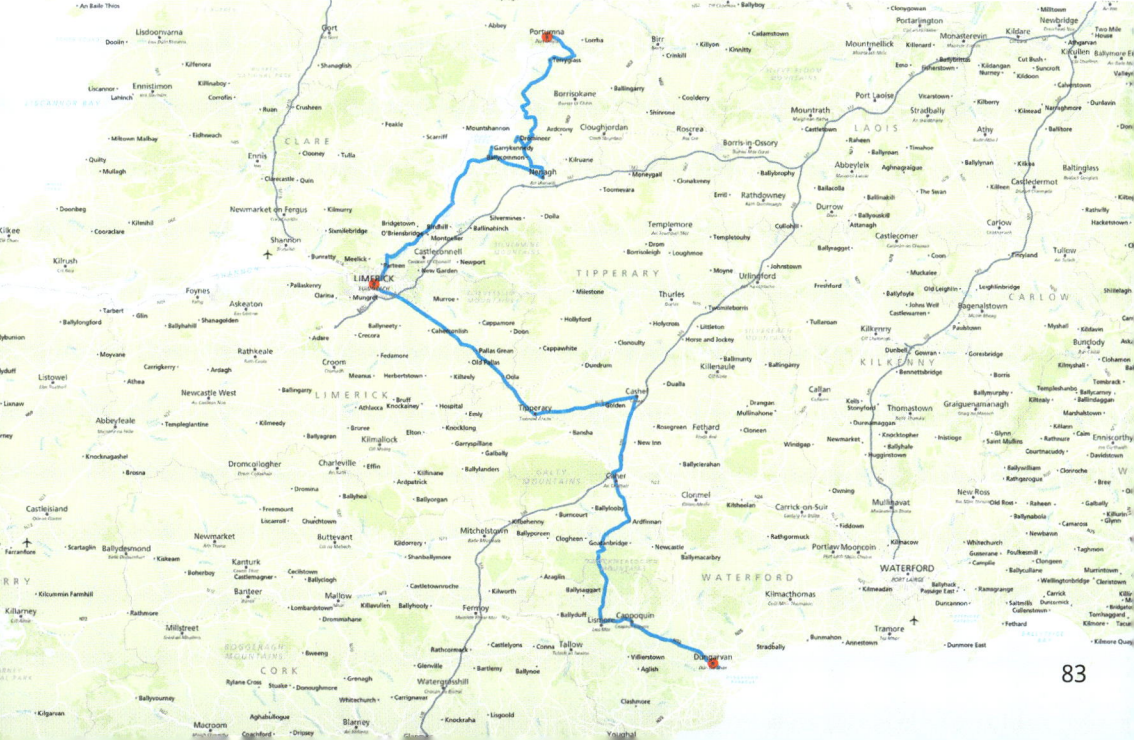

rolling hills. Turn right at Coolbaun to head for a brief pit stop at **Kilbarron Quay**, purely because it offers a beautiful view of the lake. On some days, the Lakeside Sauna pops up just down the road, where you can intersperse your sweat session with bracing dips in the lake – check the website for their days and hours.

Alternatively, if you have the time for another detour you can stop into **Dromineer** as the road carries on down – Ritual has a lakeside sauna overlooking Lough Derg, as well as a coffee truck and fireside hangout area. It has a great vantage point of the water, and you can often see windsurfers flying along its surface.

From there, head into **Nenagh**, a handsome town with the excellent **Nenagh Castle** at its centre. Free to visit (and supposedly haunted), you can climb the 101 steps right to the top of this thirteenth-century tower for great views out over the castle gardens next door and the nearby steeples. Be sure to have a chat with the OPW guide at reception, who can fill you in on the history of the tower, which was once the seat of the

Ballina town, County Mayo.

Butler family. To enter, you walk through a hole in the side that was made by a farmer in 1760, who put gunpowder in the wall to scare off the sparrows, thus blowing a hole in the process.

When it's time to hit the road, head out on the R494 back towards Lough Derg, stopping briefly in **Garrykennedy** if only to visit Larkins, a thatched pub by the water that serves top notch comfort food by the fireside. Carry on along the R494 as the road rises for excellent views of Lough Derg – there's a layby just beyond **Ballingear** that is a great place to pull in for a photo (it's marked on maps as **The Lookout**).

The road glides through the countryside until you meet **Ballina**, with County Clare's **Killaloe** just on the other side of the mouth of the lough. From there, cross over the new bypass, Brian Boru bridge (the namesake was born nearby), and make your way down to

Nenagh Castle

Brian Boru bridge.

Limerick, to spend the rest of the day (and night) exploring the city. The tiny **Treaty City Brewery** is a great spot for an IPA or ale (they also do tours on Fridays and Saturdays) and the riverside **Curragower** restaurant serve up a mean fish and chips.

Day 2 – Limerick to Dungarvan

Start your day by seeing a bit more of Limerick city – **King John's Castle** is right on the River Shannon, and there's 800 years of history to explore on a self-guided tour. Art fans will love the **Hunt Museum**, which also has some outdoor art installations, and **The People's Museum of Limerick** is set in a beautiful Georgian townhouse and explores the quirkier side of the city's history. If your visit falls on a Saturday, be sure to pop into the **Milk Market**, where there are

King John's Castle.

Rock of Cashel.

tonnes of food stands and stalls, whether you want to pick up some artisan sandwiches for later on or tuck into a pastry with a coffee before you hit the road.

From Limerick, head out of the city on the N24, driving through **Tipperary** town and heading out on the N74 to **Cashel**. The big attraction here, of course, is the **Rock of Cashel**, and that'll be your first stop. Standing tall on a jagged rock in the middle of the town, this gaggle of medieval buildings includes a twelfth-century round tower, a Romanesque chapel, a thirteenth-century Gothic cathedral and much more, along with a small space that plays an audiovisual presentation. This is where Brian Boru was crowned High King in 978.

You can opt for the guided or self-guided tours, though only the guided tours include the interior of Cormac's chapel. There's a lovely little tea room down by the car park, too. In the town of Cashel itself there are some great craft shops and the five-star hotel, the **Cashel Palace**, which also owns Mikey Ryan's on the main street, a gastropub that's a handy spot for lunch.

The next spot is barely a 15-minute drive away in **Cahir**, another pretty town dominated by the castle that stands over the river. Again, there are guided or self-guided options, where you can walk through the remains of this impressive thirteenth-century structure, one of the best-preserved castles in the country. When walking over to the entrance, be sure to look up to see the cannonball wedged in the exterior wall, and when you're leaving, walk down to the picture boards to see all of the movies that have been shot here, including *Excalibur*, *The Last Duel* and *Barry Lyndon*.

This is also a good spot for a walk, if you fancy stretching your legs. The **Suir Blueway** is a 21km off-road walking and cycling trail that weaves between **Clonmel** and **Carrick-on-Suir**, but this short section takes you from Cahir Castle along the edge of the water to **Swiss Cottage**. If you can make time for the detour (bearing in mind you'll need to walk back to the car in Cahir, unless one of your party volunteers to drive and meet you at the cottage) it's well worth it, the pretty trail running along the riverbank with wooden sculptures along the way.

Swiss Cottage is open seasonally (from March to November), and is an incredible fairytale site, with a curved thatched roof and Tudor-style exterior – to see it, even from the outside, you do have to pay the entrance fee and walk through a tunnel-style staircase. If you don't want to walk, you can drive and make the slight detour outside Cahir, crossing the bridge that leads over the river.

Back on the road, you have another treat ahead of you – The Vee Pass. Driving through the Knockmealdown Mountains, the road turns back on a steep V-shape (hence the name) with incredible views of the Golden Vale and Bay Lough. When the weather is on your side, you can see for miles and miles, and in the summer months the mountains are thick with flowering heather and rhododendrons. There are places to pull over and take in the view, too.

From there, it's about a 20-minute drive to **Lismore**, best known for its annual literary festival, beautiful castle and gardens and the weekly farmers market (held on a Sunday). While **Lismore Castle** itself isn't open to the public (unless they're renting it for the night),

Carrick-on-Suir.

Lismore Castle.

the gardens are open and stunning – the Reilig Garden, Upper Garden and Lower Garden make up over 10 acres and are the oldest cultivated gardens in Ireland. And even if you can't see the interior of the castle, the view of the structure from outside is particularly striking, the turrets and parapets standing tall alongside the Blackwater River.

Back in the car, head out on the N72 that loosely follows the river path, stopping if you please at the eighteenth-century Georgian mansion, **Cappoquin House**. You can take a tour of the property in April and May, explore the expansive gardens or stay the night in their off-grid Cabin Under The Hills, which also has a sauna.

If you're not staying, continue along the N72 and you'll end up in **Dungarvan**, a lovely spot to stay the night. Head to Paul and Máire Flynn's restaurant the **Tannery**, or get the best fish and chips you'll likely ever eat in Andchips.

Dungarvan Castle.

Dungarvan Harbour.

MUNSTER – Trip 12: 2 days
Copper Coast & East Cork

The west has the Wild Atlantic Way, the north has the Causeway Coast, but the east can often slip under the radar. However, while it doesn't have quite as snazzy a tagline or the same number of jaw-dropping white sand beaches, the Copper Coast has just as much allure. There are rugged clifftops, charming lighthouses and, crucially, a huge number of historically interesting sights along the way. This is the road trip for those who want to combine a bit of heritage and geology with some great food and a lesser-trodden patch of coastline, all the way from Wexford down into East Cork. There, the coastal road takes you up and along striking cliffs, through beautiful villages and by Irish landmarks like Ballymaloe Cookery School.

Need to Know

Duration: 2 days

Distance: 322km/200 miles

When to go: April or October

Start at: Wexford Town

Finish at: Cork

The route

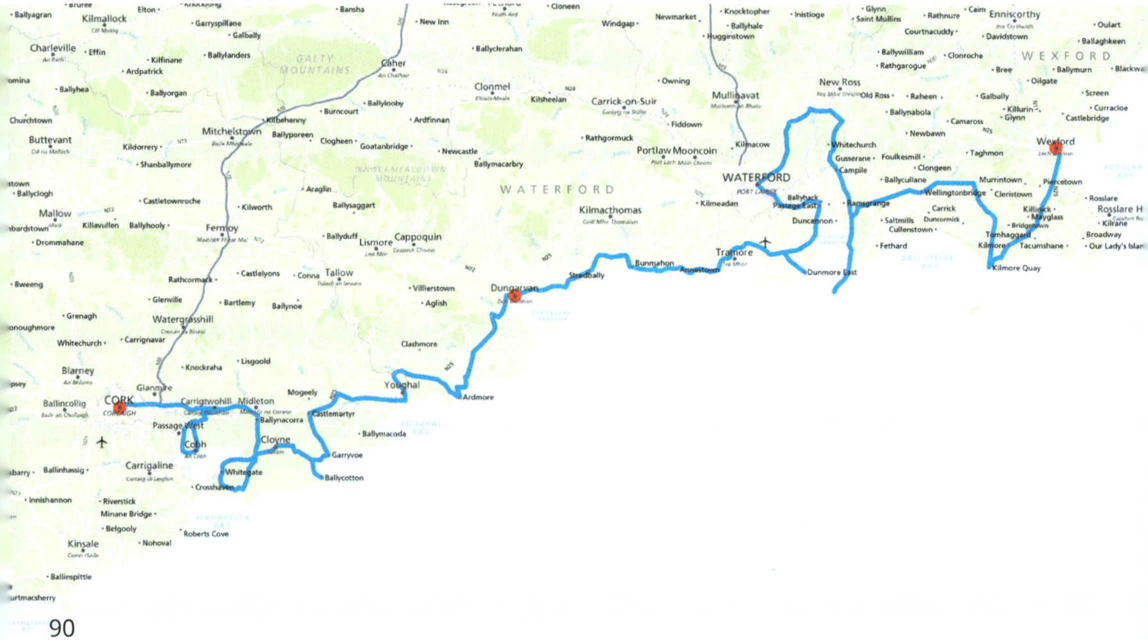

Quick view

Day 1: Start in Wexford, then head to the coast and choose from several options.

Day 2: Begin in Dungarvan, then make your way to Cork via the coast and Cobh.

Tintern Abbey, River Wye, Sandhill, County Wexford.

Day 1 – Wexford to Dungarvan

Start things off in **Wexford**, where you can take a stroll along the buildings by the edge of the water at the harbour, visit the National Opera House or try some of the local seafood restaurants. If it's open, visit the Scúp gelato stand by the harbour, for some roasted banana ice cream.

When you're ready to go, head out of town on the N25, turning off to join the R739 down towards **Kilmore Quay**, passing charming thatched cottages at the roadside along the way. This pretty fishing village is a nice spot for a stroll, but is also the departure point for boat trips out to the **Saltee Islands**. If you have the time to factor this into a trip (Kilmore Quay is about a half an hour drive from Wexford) then it's well worth popping over to the island, particularly if you're there between late April and July, when the puffins return to their burrows and hop around the long grass and clifftops. The crossing takes twenty minutes, and you have three and a half hours before it's time to return.

Back in Kilmore Quay, get some top notch fish and chips at the Saltee Chipper before you head on towards your next stop, **Tintern Abbey**. Founded in 1200, the majority of the Cistercian monastery still stands, including the nave, chancel, tower, chapel and cloister,

A Puffin returns to its nest burrow with fish, Great Saltee Island.

Hook Lighthouse.

all surrounded by woodland. There are walking trails on the grounds, as well as the nearby **Colclough Walled Garden**, restored to appear as it would have looked in the 1830s.

You'll need to head back to meet the L4041 to make your way towards the **Hook Peninsula**, passing over the old stone bridge just before Saltmills. From there, you're making your way down to the very tip of **Hook Head**, but stop first in **Fethard**, purely for a coffee and a homemade doughnut at Grálinn.

The road then weaves down the peninsula, taking you by picturesque beaches until you're on the singular track towards **Hook Lighthouse**. On the way, you'll get a look at Loftus Hall to the right, reportedly the most haunted building in Ireland. Then you're at your destination, the oldest intact operational lighthouse in the world. Dating back 800 years, Hook Lighthouse is a spectacular structure, and you can hear all about its history on a guided tour, which culminates in an

exceptional view from the very top (if you can make it up the 115 stone spiral steps, that is).

If you did want to split the road trip up (or if you were visiting the puffins on the Saltee Irelands, and wanted to tag an extra night on), it's worth bearing in mind that this is a great spot for sunset, as is the **Dollar Bay** beach you'll pass on the L4045 back up north. However, it's a lovely beach too for a stroll, as is its neighbour **Booley Beach**.

To hop over to the next headland, you have two choices – you can make your way back up to the N25 to stick to the roads, or you can take the **Passage East Car Ferry**, which runs continuously throughout the day, back and forth every ten or fifteen minutes. It's a bit of a novelty, and shaves about 20 minutes off your journey time, too.

When you've crossed over in to County Waterford, make your way down to **Dunmore East** to hop out and explore

Dollar Bay Beach.

in the nineteenth-century, the road passes by information points, castles and cliff walks, so you can hop out whenever the mood strikes or simply enjoy the view from the car.

At some points, the road glides right by the sea, rising up over verdant green cliffs and overlooking the waves. The road between Annestown and Bunmahon has some of the best coastal views, with viewpoints along the way where you can pull in, as well as beaches where you can stop. The **Copper Coast UNESCO Global Geopark** visitor centre is just beyond Bunmahon.

You can turn off the road to see the **Bunmahon Beach Viewpoint** or head to the beautiful cove of **Trá na mBó**, or you can continue along the track along the coast towards Stradbally. Make your way along the coast as you move towards **Dungarvan**, making a segue to the striking Ballyvole Cove, then moving over the Barnawee Bridge into the town.

this seaside village. There are clifftop walking trails, seaside saunas and fish and chip shops to check out, too.

From there, head back up to the R685 to follow the road to **Tramore**, where the **Copper Coast** officially begins. This UNESCO Global Geopark stretches for 25km along the Waterford coastline, roughly from Fenor to Stradbally, though the views don't stop when the official route does. Named after the copper mines that were prolific along the shore

If you do have another bit of driving in you, it's less than 20 minutes on to **Helvic**, a beautiful Gaeltacht on the Ring Peninsula with gorgeous views along the way.

Trá na mBó beach.

Otherwise, you're spoiled for choice when it comes to places to eat in Dungarvan, where seafood features heavily on many a menu and the pubs are cosy, jovial and alluring after such a long day on the road.

Day 2 – Dungarvan to Cobh

Set off from Dungarvan on the N25, making your way over the deep green fields with views of the sea on the horizon. Your target is **Ardmore**, an endlessly charming coastal village with plenty of artsy boutiques, coffee shops and an excellent cliff top walk. Grab a coffee and make your way up to the **Ardmore Cliff Path**, walking as far as you please (the full loop is just under 4km and should take about an hour). Along the way, you'll pass a Napoleonic era look out post and the fifth-century site of St Declan's Well, as well as the

incredible views over Ardmore Bay and out to the ocean.

From there, continue along the road to **Youghal**, making a detour at **Goat Island Beach** to see this beautiful sheltered bay. Back on the road, you'll cross over the bridge into County Cork, swinging down the coastline and inland until you reach Shannagrry, home to **Ballymaloe Cookery School**. This where many top chefs made their name, but it's worth a stop to pick up something delicious (and freshly baked) in the shop, and take a walk around their extensive gardens – don't miss Shell House, a folly plastered with thousands of shells.

Rejoin the coast as you meet **Ballycotton**, for one of the finest cliff walks in the country. This 9km walk isn't exactly a quick stroll, but if you're a hiker you'll be in for a treat, the clifftop trail

Ardmore Cliff.

Milky Way over Ballycotton.

weaving alongside thick heather and overlooking the crashing waves below – you may even spot the local dolphins, if you're lucky. You get a great view of the **Ballycotton Lighthouse**, too.

The road then moves along the East Cork shore, where you'll pause at **Inch Beach** if you want a better look at the sea, before looping around the headland via Whitegate and moving up to **Midleton**. The main attraction here is the **Midleton Distillery Experience**, where Jameson (as well as other premium whiskey brands) are made. The tour is fascinating, moving through all of their old stone buildings, and culminating in a tasting (if you're the one behind the wheel, there are non-alcoholic alternatives and you can pick up a bottle in the shop for later on).

There's also an excellent farmer's market in Midleton on Saturdays, if you want to pick up some local produce, fresh sourdough and other treats.

When you're ready to depart, join the N25 to make your way towards Cork city, but turn off when the road reaches Slatty Water to drive down the R624 towards Cobh. This road skirts around **Fota Island**, home to the expansive wildlife park and the Regency mansion Fota House, with its delightful gardens and arboretum.

Head on the L289 towards **Cobh**, a picturesque seaside town with brightly coloured houses that slope down towards the sea, with the gothic St Colman's Cathedral standing guard. Walk up to the 'Deck of Cards' houses for a quintessential view of both, and pop into the Titanic Experience Cobh if you have the time. This is the very last spot where the Titanic saw land before meeting its fate in the Atlantic, and this tiny museum tells the story of the people who docked (and luckily disembarked) here. This is also where boats set off for Spike Island, the nearby island that's been a prison, a monastery and a fortress over the past 1300 years.

Aerial view of St Anne's Church and
Cathedral in Shandon, Cork.

To continue, follow the R264, a scenic road that hugs the shoreline, and brings you back to meet the N25. From there, follow the same road all the way into **Cork** city, where you'll wrap up this epic trip.

There is, of course, plenty to see and do in Cork, from the well-known landmarks like the **Shandon bells** in **St Anne's Church** to the **English Market**, possibly the best food market in the Republic of Ireland. You can also walk through the pretty grounds of University College Cork to find the **Lewis Glucksman Gallery**, or set off on a boat trip through **Cork Harbour,** which takes you all the way along the **River Lee** until you meet the sea, giving you a whole new view of Cobh (it does, admittedly, look even more impressive from the water).

Cork Harbour with the town of Cobh on the skyline.

English Market, Cork.

MUNSTER – Trip 13: 1 day
Inland West Cork

West Cork gets a lot of attention for its coastline – and quite rightfully so. However, focusing on the Wild Atlantic Way along means missing a whole heap of what makes this region so great – peaceful forests with walking trails galore, villages with less of a tourist track and moments of natural beauty so striking, you don't even miss the sea. This one-day trip focuses on the inland highlights of West Cork, including the Muscraí Gaeltacht, and goes at a leisurely pace – you could also wrap up the route in less than a day, if you'd prefer. Alternatively, you can easily tag it onto one of the coastal routes in the region, like the Ring of Kerry (see page 42), which can be taken from Kenmare, or the Sheep's Head and Beara Peninsula route, which ends up in Kenmare after the first day (see page 60).

Need to Know

Duration: 1 day

Distance: 134km/83 miles

When to go: May to June

Start at: Cork

Finish at: Kenmare

The route

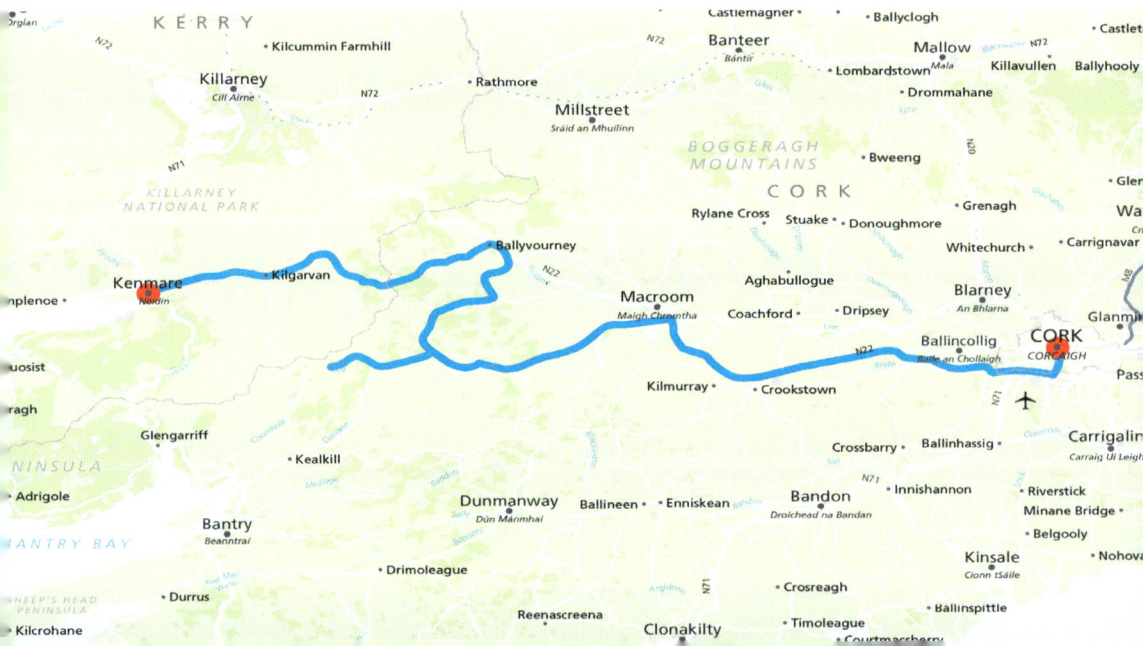

Quick view

Day 1: Head out from Cork city across the belly of the county towards Gougane Barra, loosely following the River Lee and passing alongside lakes and nature reserves, finishing up in Kenmare.

Shakey Bridge, Cork.

If you have some time to spare before you leave **Cork city**, there are several things you can do that won't take up too much of the day. Head out to the riverside **Fitzgerald Park**, where you can stroll around the 18 acres of peaceful gardens, see the Sky Garden (for which Diarmuid Gavin won an award at the Chelsea Flower Show) and take a walk over what's known locally as the Shakey Bridge, due to its movement underfoot.

Nano Nagle Place is a handy spot on the right side of the city for a departure – this museum tells the story of Nano Nagle, a pioneering woman who devoted her life to helping the poor, and opened seven schools around Cork for the children who were denied an education. There are usually a few different exhibitions on, one with more of an arts focus, and the grounds are beautiful, too. Be sure to get breakfast or brunch in the Good Day and Nádúr Deli, a space overlooking the gardens that serves exceptional food with a South Pacific flavour.

When you're ready, head out of the city on Friars Walk, heading south to find the N40, which soon becomes the N22. After a while, you'll rediscover the River Lee, which broadens out just before you hit **Macroom**. Just outside the village is **The Gearagh**, a

The Gearagh, a submerged glacial woodland.

nature reserve that was formed at the end of the last Ice Age. Take a look at the water and you'll see the gnarled old stumps of oak trees – until 1954, this area was an oak forest, the last surviving one of its kind in Western Europe. However, it was flooded to enable the construction of hydroelectric dams. Now, it's a haunting reminder of what once stood there for centuries.

At the other side, you'll meet **Toonsbridge**, known best for the excellent cheese made by **Toonsbridge Dairy**, using milk from their herd of buffalo. Their set-up in the village is a great spot to stop, where you can browse the cheeses they make right on site, or the produce grown in their garden next door. They serve pizza at the weekends, too.

From Toonsbridge, head out on the R584, which loosely follows the trail of the River Lee – there's a pretty riverside stop, the **Inchigeela Boat Slip**, if you want a nice view of the water and the mountains, and the river briefly blends

Gougane Barra Lake.

into Lough Allua, which you drive alongside.

When you reach Ballingeary, continue on the R584, taking a very brief detour to **The Stepping Stones** if you wish. Turn off to the right when you see the big religious statue, and you'll soon be at **Gougane Barra**. This iconic landmark

Rowing boats on the lake near the small church at St Finbarr's Oratory, Ballingeary.

the L3402 and follow the meandering country road up north until you turn left onto Reannanerre. You'll turn right on Rath East, briefly following the line of the River Douglas, until you reach the village of **Ballyvourney**. If you're a beer drinker, call into 9 White Deer brewery (known locally as Fia Bán) to pick up some of their concoctions for later on.

They're named after the nearby site of Baile Bhuirne, where St Gobnait later established an abbey – according to a sixth-century fable, she was told she would see nine white deer and discover a mystical well. That site is just a mile or so down the road, and you can both visit the holy well and **St Gobnait's Forest**, where there are walking trails through the woodland.

On the other side of the village, turn left at Mills Inn to drive through **Coolea** (there's an outdoor swimming pool just off the road, Linn Snámha Chúil Aodha, if you fancy a swim in the summer months). From there, the road moves up into the mountains, and almost as

is the highlight of the Muscraí Gaeltacht, a picture-perfect valley surrounded by mountains and forests, and one of the best-known views is of the nineteenth-century St Finbarr's Oratory, which sits on a tiny spit of land in the Gougane Barra Lake.

It's a beautiful sight throughout the year, particularly when it's calm and the water acts like a mirror, reflecting the surrounding bulbous mountains and the oratory itself. But it comes into its own in the autumn, when the hills and woodlands are bursting in hues of amber and maroon as the leaves change.

There are six walking trails in the **Gougane Barra Forest Park**, where you can park up and head out for a hike. These routes vary from 30-minute walks to more strenuous two hour hikes, and the trailheads for all can be found in the car park or online at Coillte.

When you're back in the car, drive back along the road you came on until you meet Ballingeary, then turn left on

St Finbarr's oratory on an island in the lake in Gougane Barra.

soon as you cross the boundaries into County Kerry you'll find **Top of Coom**, Ireland's highest pub. You'll carry along this rolling mountain road, with thick boulders either side, as you meet the River Roughty and then turn left onto the R569.

You'll pass through Kilgarvan (which is Healy Rae country – you'll drive right by Healy Rae's Bar) and the dense Kerry countryside, before you reach the mouth of **Kenmare Bay** and finish up in the town itself.

However, if you did want to drive back to Cork that evening, you can drive the straight route from **Kenmare**, mostly following the N22. That will take you roughly an hour and a half, depending on traffic.

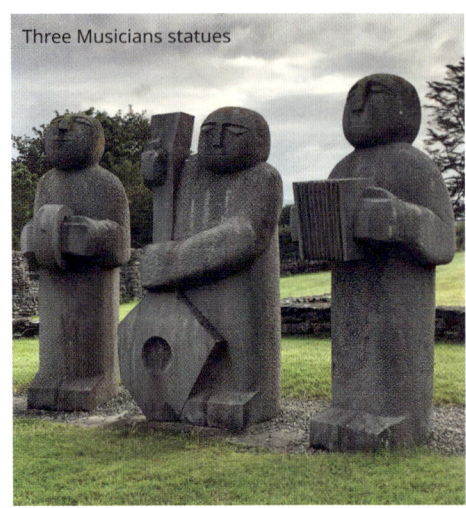

Three Musicians statues

Kenmare Bay.

Henry Street, Kenmare.

ULSTER – Trip 14: 2 days
Causeway Coast

Possibly Ireland's second most famous shoreline drive, the Causeway Coastal Route hugs the edge of the water from just outside Belfast all the way up and over to Derry, taking in some incredible sights along the way. The drive, along a road that clings to the northern coast, weaves through tiny tunnels cut into stone and takes you up and over mountains, and it's enough of an experience in itself. But there's joy too to be found in stopping frequently along the way, to challenge your nerves on a rope bridge that swings high over the crashing waves, or to see the (many) filming locations from *Game of Thrones*. This is definitely one to spread out over two days, but you can stretch it out if you want to spend less time behind the wheel and more time out and about.

Need to Know

Duration: 2 days

Distance: 224km/139 miles

When to go: October, when the weather is chilly

Start at: Belfast

Finish at: Derry

The route

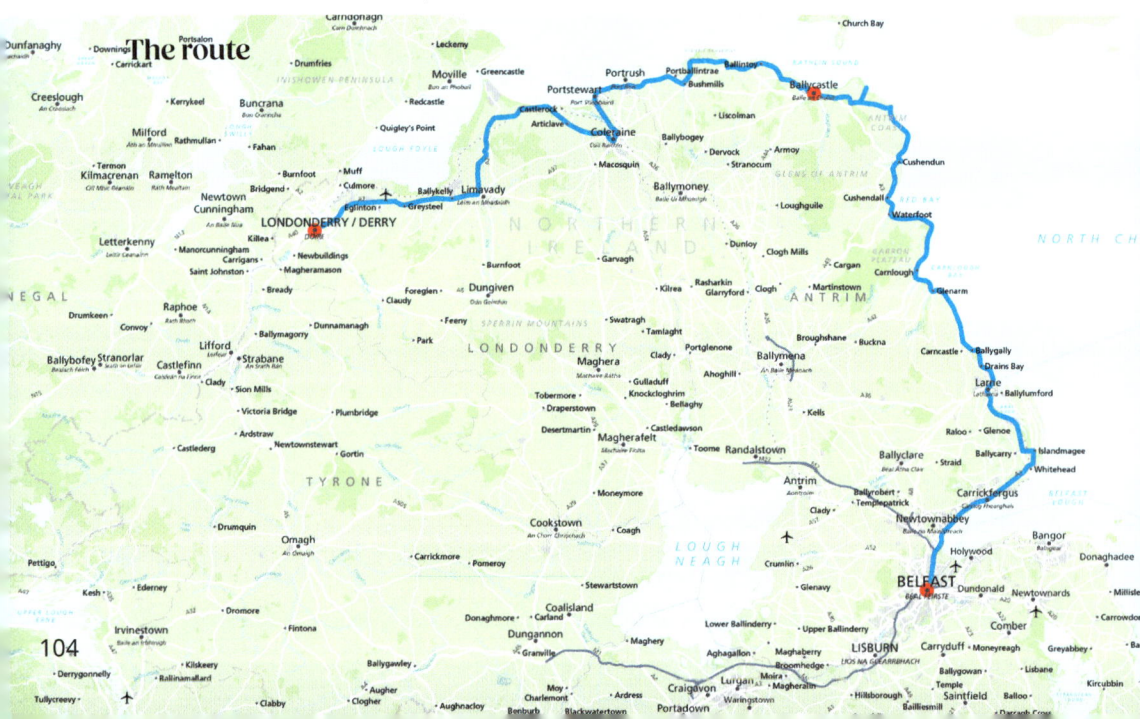

Quick view

Day 1: Drive from Belfast all the way up the eastern coastline of Northern Ireland, stopping for the night in Ballycastle.

Day 2: Hit the road and drive along the northern shore until you wind up in Derry.

Day 1 – Belfast to Ballycastle

Before you set off, you'll likely want to spend a bit of time exploring **Belfast** – if you do, be sure to allow another day (or a good few hours, at least) as the first proper day of driving includes more scenic stops than you may expect.

Titanic Belfast is a must-see in the city, with an immersive, multimedia experience that takes you through every element of the infamous ship, from its construction right on this very spot (the museum is set on what was the shipyard) all the way through to the moment it sank, and the aftermath. There's a moving monument to those who passed away in the disaster, and a mesmerising floating replica of the ship that rotates above an exhibition of items recovered from the ship, like a pocket watch owned by Malcolm Joakim Johnson, the hands of which are frozen at the very moment the ship sank.

In the city proper, head to **St George's Market** if you're there at the weekend, to tuck into all the excellent regional cuisine, then check out the street art that's peppered around the middle of town – you can also take a tour led by artists with **Seed Head Arts**.

Titanic Belfast.

Carrickfergus Castle and Belfast Lough.

When you're ready to leave Belfast, it doesn't take long to find the Causeway Coastal Route. Leave the city on the M2 then follow the M5, then take the Shore Road to drive along the water's edge at **Belfast Lough**. This road takes you right past **Carrickfergus Castle**, a Norman stronghold right on the water, which you can explore throughout the year.

The Gobbins Cliff Path.

Continue on this road briefly, until you see the turning for **The Gobbins**, a Victorian coastal route that takes you right up to the edge of these dramatic cliffs. There's only one problem – a route this rugged is subject to the power of the elements, and due to numerous rockfalls over the years it's actually been closed more often than it's been open, since they relaunched in 2015. Check ahead though, because if it is open when you visit it's an exhilarating experience – you're guided on a walk along a series of different platforms and tunnels, taking you right up close to the rocks and their resident seabirds, as the waves smash to your other side.

When you're back on the Shore Road, you'll swing through **Larne** before hitting the main Coast Road, with slopes of gorse-lined bushes to your left and the sea to your right. It's a striking portion of road, particularly when you drive through the **Black Arch**, where the road cuts right through the rock in a tunnel made in the nineteenth-century.

The road continues to glide along the shore, between rocky sections and muddy sand beaches, curving towards **Ballygally** – keep an eye out for O'Haloran's Castle on the right, sticking up on a jagged little island. Just after, you'll drive through Ballygally itself, with the **Ballygally Castle Hotel** a good stopping point for either ghost fans (it's supposedly haunted) or *Game of Thrones* nuts (they have one of the ten ornately illustrated doors inside, which were carved from trees from the Dark Hedges that fell during a storm).

The road continues along the water (with views of Wales to your right, on a clear day) and up to **Glenarm**, where you can make a pit stop at the castle and grounds, if you fancy a break. Otherwise,

carry on up through **Carnlough** up to **Cushendall**, where you can pause to stretch your legs at **Cushendall Beach**. The next stop is another for *Game of Thrones* fans – the caves at Cushendun were showcased on the series when Melisandre birthed a shadow demon. And if that means nothing to you, don't worry – the caves are impressive enough on their own. They're just a short walk from where you can park up, but are occasionally closed due to bad weather, so be cautious.

From there, the road starts to rise up, giving you an elevated view of the water, with the occasional field of sheep to your right leading down to the sea. You're now technically on the **Torr Head Scenic Route**, which is a decent drive in and of itself, but be sure to turn off to drive straight to **Torr Head** itself, which gives an incredible lookout spot over the water and all the way to Scotland, the jagged line of rocky tendrils on the coast creeping in and out of the sea.

Torr Head on the Causeway Coastal Route, County Antrim.

You can also turn off to check out **Murlough Bay**, purely because it's pretty. You get a good view of **Rathlin Island** there, too. Back on the main track, the road swings inland slightly until you reach **Ballycastle**, which is a good stopping point for the night. It's well known for its trad music, so you can follow your nose between the pubs that line the harbour to find some good sessions, or take the more formal Ballycastle Traditional Music Trail. If you're sticking around for another night, there are also numerous boat trips that set off from the harbour, whether you want to do some fishing or head out to Rathlin Island – the ferries do technically take cars, but you're better off parking on the mainland and exploring on foot when you're over there.

Day 2 – Ballycastle to Derry

Start the day off by picking up some provisions in **Ursa Minor**, a bakehouse that's known for its exceptional sourdough (they supply many of the top restaurants in Northern Ireland with their loaves).

The road weaves up towards **Ballintoy**, but your first stop should be the **Carrick-a-Rede Rope Bridge**. Connecting the mainland to a tiny, rocky island, this rope bridge was first erected in 1755 and swings almost 100 feet over the sea, swaying in the breeze (it's closed in high winds, for obvious reasons). Even if you don't have a fear of heights, it's an exhilaratingly nervy experience, looking down at the swirling sea far, far below. When you're over on the island, you can take a little walk to see the fisherman's

Ballycastle Harbour.

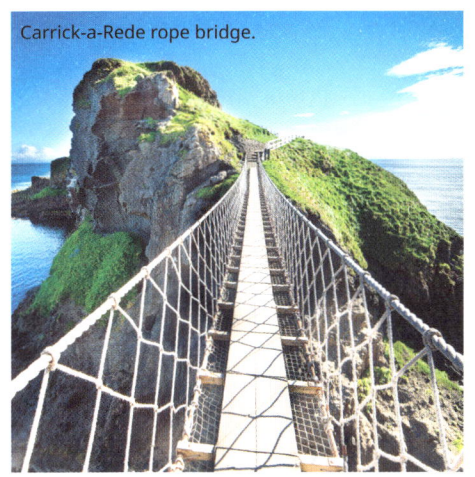

Carrick-a-Rede rope bridge.

cottage, before returning the same way you came.

Soon after, the slaloming road takes you to **Ballintoy**, where you should make a beeline for the harbour (at the risk of overkill, this too was featured in *Game of Thrones*). When you're back on the road, you'll find it's a little further back from the sea but no less beautiful. You'll pass by the car park for **White Park Bay**, a beautiful cliff-lined beach that can only

be reached on foot – it's about a mile and a half from the car park, and you may well be joined by the local farmer's cows when you get to the sands.

Be sure you don't miss the turning back to the Causeway Road, where the scenery soon gets dramatic. You'll pass by **Dunseverick Castle,** the remnants of a promontory fort right on the edge of the cliffs. There's more to see if you're interested, like the **Dunseverick Falls** and natural pool, but if not, continue inland until you reach the village of **Bushmills**.

It's a pretty village, but of course that's not what it's known for. Bushmills is the world's oldest licensed whiskey distillery, in operation since 1608. Even if you're not a whiskey drinker, it's a fascinating place to tour, between the old stone buildings and the story of the wooden casks still made by the families of coopers who handcraft each barrel today. If you wanted to avail of the tasting, you could stay in Bushmills for the night rather than Ballycastle – **Bushmills Inn** is a lovely, cosy choice.

Dunseverick Castle.

Dunluce Castle.

Your first stop is a very short drive away – **Dunluce Castle**. The romantic remains of the sixteenth-century castle clings to the edge of the craggy headland, mostly a shell but with a lot of the primary architecture intact. Take a walk through and you can see former remnants, like old fireplaces and window frames, and get an exceptional view down the cliffs to the sea below. There are also little wildflowers that grow only here, with tiny yellow petals. Look further along the shoreline and you may catch a glimpse of the **Wishing Arch**, too.

Back on the Dunluce Road, you'll drive along the clifftops passing the white sands of **White Rocks Beach**, before hitting the town of **Portrush**. You'll pass right by the Dunluce Links course of the **Royal Portrush Golf Club**, which has hosted the Open several times, most

recently in 2025. Portrush town is a good spot for a quick stroll and a spot of lunch, or you can walk out along the Ramore Head walking trails if you want something a bit more scenic.

Soon after you leave, you'll meet another handsome Victorian beach town, **Portstewart**. If you haven't already eaten, then go to **Harry's Shack**, one of the best restaurants in Northern Ireland, serving fresh seafood right on the sands of Portstewart Strand.

From there, the road curves back in to pass through **Coleraine**, until it rejoins the coast at **Downhill**. Stop just before to see **Mussenden Temple** on the grounds of the eighteenth-century Downhill Demesne, the pinnacle of which is the incredible temple built right on top of the cliffs, with a fantastic view down to the beach below. You can't go inside, but you can walk around this and the grounds themselves, where you can also see the remains of the original mansions.

You won't say goodbye to the sea views entirely, but it does get a little less exciting as the road gets closer to **Derry**, on the A2. However, there's plenty to see and do in this little city, from walking the ancient city walls (past the giant mural of the TV sensation *Derry Girls*) to crossing the peace bridge over to the **Treaty City Brewery**, where you can tuck into a big plate of gastropub favourites while sampling a tipple or two of their own ales, to celebrate coming to the end of the Causeway Coast.

Peace Bridge, Derry

ULSTER – Trip 15: 2 days
Inland Northern Ireland

Fancy an epic, two-day trip across the width of Northern Ireland? This trip takes in some of the highlights of the region, from the scenic Sperrin Mountains to the Lakelands in Fermanagh, by way of ancient country estates, mountains and Dark Sky stargazing reserves. You can, of course, chop and change the routes, doing just one of the days or all three, but whatever you choose you'll soak in some of the best scenery, towns and sights that Northern Ireland has to offer.

Need to Know

Duration: 2 days

Distance: 417km/259 miles

When to go: Spring, when the wildflowers are blooming

Start at: Belfast

Finish at: Enniskillen

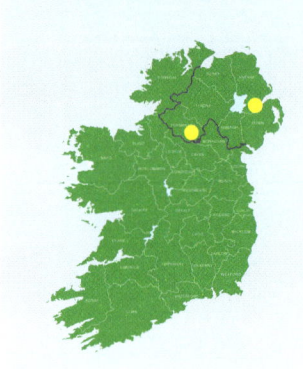

The route

Quick view

Day 1: Travel from Belfast out over the Sperrins, calling in at Hillsborough Castle, the Ulster American Folk Park and the Om Dark Sky Reserve, before you reach Enniskillen.

Day 2: Drive a loop from Enniskillen taking in the Fermanagh Lakelands, the Marble Arch Caves and the Cuilcagh Boardwalk.

Day 1 – Belfast to Enniskillen

This trips kicks off in **Belfast**, and you can find some tips for what to do in the city on page 105. Firstly, make your way to the M1 and head south out of the city, passing by Lisburn before heading to your first stop, **Royal Hillsborough**. This small village has the look of something knocked up by a Disney movie crew, with its quaint shopfronts, ivy-covered buildings and arched coach houses.

The big attraction is **Hillsborough Castle and Gardens**, the official residence of the UK royal family in Northern Ireland. It's a magnificent structure even from the gates, but you can also take a tour of the state rooms that are in use, like the throne room, drawing rooms and Stair Hall, with a cantilevered stone stair that dates back to 1797.

There are also 100 acres of grounds and gardens to explore, with rare trees and plants, a yew tree walk and Lady Alice's Temple, first built in 1867. This is where Mo Mowlam sat in contemplation during her work Secretary of State for Northern Ireland, when she worked on the Good Friday Agreement and lived at Hillsborough Castle.

Outside of the castle gates, the village is a nice place for a wander – head down to **Hillsborough Forest** to

Hillsborough Castle.

Aerial photo of Beaghmore Neolithic
Stone Circles County Tyrone.

walk the Lake Trail, which leads you through the woodland and around the lakeshore. If you're peckish, there are some artisan bakeries and gastropubs on the main village drag.

From there, find your way back to the M1 and head west, following the path to the Sperrin Mountains. If you have an interest in historic houses, call in first to **The Argory**, a neo-classical mansion now run by the National Trust, with a beautiful rose garden, walking trails and a courtyard café.

Turn off the A4 at Cabragh, and you'll then head into the foothills of the Sperrins. After about half an hour,

you'll pass the **Beaghmore Stone Circles Landmark**, which were discovered in the 1920s. There are 7 stone circles, 10 rows of stones and 12 cairns, which are believed to date back to neolithic times. And, like Newgrange, it's believed there was a knowledge of astronomy entwined in their creation, which makes it all the more apt that the **Om Dark Sky Park** is just a short drive away – there's even a Solar Walk which links the stone circle and the modern day observatory.

Even if you're driving during the day, it's worth calling into the visitor centre, where there's an interactive exhibition, holographic installation and guided tours, as well as events like forest bathing.

Ulster American Folk Park.

From there, carry on driving up and through the Sperrins, passing **Sawel Mountain**, the highest peak, and **Lough Ash** to the north. If you want to, take the brief detour to drive down to Barnes Gap, but bear in mind the road is very, very narrow.

After passing through Strabane, you'll get to the **Ulster American Folk Park**. The concept may seem unusual, but this outdoor museum tells the fascinating story of the two million people who emigrated from Northern Ireland and headed to America in the eighteenth and nineteenth centuries. There's a full-size emigrant ship, old thatched cottages and crafting demonstrations, as well as a regular rotation of exhibitions on display.

From there, it's less than an hour to **Enniskillen**, where you can park up and stay for the night. If you fancy a pint, **Blakes of the Hollow** is a lovely Victorian pub that's been on the go since 1887. They serve great food upstairs at 28 of the Hollow, too.

Day 2

There's not quite as much driving today (though there is a hefty hike included in the schedule – more on that later). So if you want to spend a bit of time exploring **Enniskillen**, head to the castle, where you can flit between small museums, see the castle and visit the little artisan shops at the **Butter Market**.

Enniskillen Catle.

Bronze age stone carving of a man on one side and a woman on the other.
They are located in Caldragh Cemetery on Boa Island, Lower Lough Erne.

If you have two hours to spare, a boat trip up **Lough Erne** to **Devenish Island** is a must – on a trip with Erne Tours, you'll glide up the beautiful Lower Lough Erne, past swaying rushes and wildlife until you reach this monastic site, which was established in the sixth century. Now, there are well preserved round towers, a fifteenth-century stone cross and the ruins of an Augustinian abbey.

When leaving Enniskillen, you'll pass by the lower lake on the Lough Shore Road, with the water slipping in and out of view as you move further north. By the time you hit the Boa Island Road, those views in full force, the road taking you right over the top of the water with an excellent vantage point of all the tiny lake isles along the way. You'll drive through **Boa Island**, passing the private **Lusty Beg Island** as well, before rejoining the mainland.

If you're looking for a quirky place to stay, or an interesting spa experience, **Finn Lough** and its unique bubble domes are just around the corner – but bear in mind it's otherwise closed for visitors and any experiences must be booked in advance.

The lake views continue as you carry on along Boa Island Road, which weaves you through the Fermanagh countryside until you reach **Belleek**. The big draw here is **Belleek Pottery**, where they've been making their distinctive fine china since 1849. You can take a tour of the facilities, going into the factory itself, then check out the extensive shop and tea room.

Now, the next option does add about 40 minutes to your total drive time, but is worth it if you want a fabulous vantage point of Lough Erne. You'll head back along the south of the lake (though

An aerial view over Lough Erne.

be careful not to take the Lough Shore Road, which will take you at water level). Instead, you'll leave Belleek on the B52, then turn off onto the Cornahaltie Road until you reach Correl Glen for the **Lough Navar Forest Drive**. You'll then drive a loop up to the **Cliffs of Magho Viewpoint**, passing the car park for **Blackslee Waterfall** along the way – if you do want to get out and see the falls, bear in mind it's a four mile loop. Otherwise, you'll get a cracking view of the lake from the Cliffs of Magho.

Back on the road, you'll follow Glennasheevar Road then the snaking Tully Road back south to rejoin the B52. You'll drive along the edge of Lough MacNean Upper, passing the excellent **Corralea Adventure Centre**, if you're into kayaking or watersports.

You'll then pop briefly into the Republic at Blacklion, then back into the North to get to your next stop, the **Marble Arch Caves**. Beneath these rolling hills, you can discover 340 million years of history in a complex labyrinth of caves, sinkholes and subterranean rivers. On a guided tour, you'll be led safely underground to

Cuilcagh Mountain Park, Legnabrocky Trail.

see the illuminated caves up close, with pools, rock formations and tunnels. You can sometimes book an underground boat trip, too. Bear in mind the caves are closed after periods of heavy rainfall, so it's always best to check in advance.

Afterwards, it's just a minute's drive to another of the region's top attractions, the **Cuilcagh Boardwalk** – otherwise known as the **Stairway to Heaven**. There are two ways to access it, but the easiest

Marble Arch Caves.

to climb to its peak. At the start of the trail, you'll pass by ancient blanket bog and derelict cottages, before the peak of Cuilcagh Mountain comes into view. As you start your ascent, the trail switches to a narrow boardwalk, which winds its way up the mountain. The namesake steps appear at the very end, and may make you wonder why it's not nicknamed the Stairway to Hell. But the steep steps are worth it when you get to the top, with an incredible view of the Fermanagh countryside.

Most people allow about two to three hours to complete the walk, so factor that into your day.

When you're back down on solid ground, head out on Marble Arch Road, calling into **Florence Court** on the way – it's a ten minute drive from the Cuilcagh car park. This beautiful eighteenth-century house has one of the oldest yew trees in Ireland on its grounds, extensive walled gardens and a charming tea room – you've earned a coffee and a slab of cake after all those steps.

From there, head back into Enniskillen, less than a 20-minute drive away.

way is by using the privately owned car park, which starts right by the trailhead. Otherwise, you can park for free at **Killykeegan Nature Reserve** (where there are also toilets) but it is another mile from the trailhead – considering the full walk is 7 miles (11km) in total, you may prefer to pay for the luxury.

The **Cuilcagh Boardwalk Trail** was built to protect the delicate bogland on the mountain, but to still allow people

Florence Court House, and lawn, at Enniskillen, Co. Fermanagh.

ULSTER – Trip 16: 1 day

Mourne Coastal Route

The Mourne Mountains have long been a source of artistic inspiration, whether it was spurring C.S. Lewis to create the magical land of Narnia, or Percy French to write the poem 'The Mountains of Mourne'. So it should come as no surprise to learn that this landscape makes for an excellent road trip, combining these staggeringly beautiful mountains with a striking shoreline. The Mourne Coastal Route spans the length of the shore from Newcastle up to Newry, but it's also an ideal launching pad for the Slieve Gullion Scenic Drive, a short stretch that weaves up through the forests of the Ring of Gullion. Put them both together and you have an epic road trip for a solid day behind the wheel. This is also a fantastic route for a family road trip, calling into two spots that have excellent outdoor facilities for kids.

Need to Know

Duration: 1 day

Distance: 145km/90 miles

When to go: Summer, when Slieve Gullion is in bloom

Start at: Newcastle

Finish at: Newcastle

The route

Quick view

Day 1: Make your way out of Newcastle on the Mourne Coastal Route, passing along the shore until you detour to drive the Slieve Gullion Scenic Forest Drive, finishing up back in Newcastle by way of two other forest parks

Slieve Donard Hotel, Newcastle, County Down.

Slieve Donard, from Dundrum, near Newcastle, County Down.

This route kicks off in the seaside town of **Newcastle**, which has a classic, beach resort vibe – there's a long promenade walk, shops selling buckets and spades and people taking a dip no matter what the weather is doing. There are plans afoot to relaunch the old rock pool too, a natural seawater pool that was a huge hit in the 1920s.

The gothic redbrick **Slieve Donard** hotel stands proudly on one end of the beach, with the actual peak of **Slieve Donard** itself at the other end. It's a great place to stay, following an extensive renovation – otherwise, Newcastle is about an hour's drive from Belfast, or two and a half hours from Dublin.

When you leave Newcastle, you'll first follow the line of the seaside promenade, driving past the Victorian houses that stand along the beach. This is also the A2, or the **Mourne Coastal Route**, so you'll be following that path all the way along the coastline. As the road cuts slightly inland, you'll notice the gentle peaks starting to form as you move into the foothills of Slieve Donard, before you start to hit other coastal villages and towns along the way.

The road moves from the water's edge up to a height overlooking the ocean, but you get some epic views of the sea as you move along the coast. At some stages, the road cuts a bit further in to bring you through spots like **Kilkeel**, but when you turn right on Benagh Road you'll find your way back to the water, the road practically on the sand.

Just after this section, there's an option for a slight detour that will appeal mostly to chocoholics. Turn right on the Newry Road towards Lisnacree and you'll soon find **Neary Nógs**, an artisanal chocolate shop that specialises in stoneground dark chocolates and interesting flavour blends. You can take a mini tour of the facilities, watching them grind the cacao into a silky smooth blend, while you learn about their raw sourced cacao beans and butter. Even if you don't do the tour, the items you can buy in the shop make it worth the quick detour – it's less than a minute off the main road.

Door into a fairy house at the fairy trail, Slieve Gullion.

Back on that coastal road, you'll drive through **Killowen** and **Rostrevor**, the road following the line of the shore and dipping right back to the water again. Soon though, that water will change to that of **Carlingford Lough**, which is fed by the Newry River you'll drive alongside as you head into the town of the same time.

Aerial photo of King John's Castle on Carlingford Lough, County Louth.

Slieve Gullion Forest Park.

This is where the Mourne Coastal Route would loop back through **Newry** and over the mountainous countryside back to Newcastle. But our route takes you along the Dublin Road, then turning off on the B113 to head towards another of Northern Ireland's most beautiful road trips, the **Slieve Gullion Scenic Forest Drive**.

It may only take you 20 minutes in the car (if you don't make any stops, that is), but this route is one of the most scenic around, with incredible payoffs when it comes to views. You'll drive one way (and slowly) along the winding, very narrow trail, which bends and weaves through the tall trees of the forest and by epic views out over the Armagh valleys and Carlingford Lough. The road frequently feels like it's clinging right to the edge of the mountain, with incredible sloping fields to the side of your car. If you're driving in the summer, you'll get to see all of the heather and wild fuchsias blooming in a glorious shade of purple.

While you can't just stop wherever you please along the Forest Drive, there are plenty of places to pull in and take in the view properly, so make use of those stopping points whenever you see them pop up.

And if you want a slower, more organic experience, you can always opt to hop out at the start and walk the same route (or do it on two wheels, if you brought a bike with you). That's worth bearing in mind when you're driving, too – you'll spot many a hiker and cyclist along the way.

If you're road tripping with kids, then they're in for a treat – in **Slieve Gullion Forest Park**, there's an adventure trail called Fionn's Giant Adventure in the Hawthorne Hill Forest Nature Reserve, a Fairy Walk and an Adventure Playground, with a picnic area, climbing frames and a mini zip line.

When you're finished with the Scenic Drive (or done with the adventure ground), this route brings you down on a jagged loop to meet the road where you joined, so follow that same path out until you're in Newry. There's not too much to see in the town itself, so head straight out

Foley's Bridge, built in 1787, located in Tolleymore Forest Park.

on the rest of the Mourne Coastal Route, which takes the countryside route back to Newcastle.

Hilltown Road becomes Newry Road, as you pass through the rolling green hills and through residential areas until you reach the right turn onto the Dublin Road, which takes you right along the edge of **Lough Island Reavey Reservoir**. Soon after, you'll turn into **Castlewellan Forest Park**, with an impressive Victorian castle, a Life Adventure Centre, loads of walking trails a gigantic Peace Maze, one of the largest permanent hedge mazes in the world, which was designed to represent a peaceful future in Northern Ireland.

The **Castlewellan Arboretum** is hugely impressive too, with plenty of rare trees and plants around the gardens, which date back to the 1850s. You can walk the mile-long loop around the lakeshore, too.

When you're finished up, the drive

back down to Newcastle is barely ten minutes, but if you have another little trip in you then head to **Tollymore Forest Park**. As opposed to Castlewellan, this one is all about gloriously natural walking trails, from short, half-mile loops to longer hikes. If you have it in you, the 5.5 mile (9km) Mountain Trail is a beautiful hike, taking you through rich beech woodlands and over pretty rivers, with occasional views of the mountains.

When you're back in Newcastle and looking out for a good dinner spot, **J.J. Farrall's** (Slieve Donard's fine dining restaurant) is excellent, as is their more casual pub, the **Percy French**. The **Avoca Hotel** on the seafront also has a cosy restaurant (that was formerly a pub) and they serve great gastropub fare.

Castlewellan Forest Park, Mourne Mountains, County Down.

ULSTER – Trip 17: 1 day
Strangford Lough and *Game of Thrones*

Barely a 30 minute drive from Belfast, Strangford Lough is a serene, beguiling corner of Northern Ireland, where you can drive around the lakeshore, call into historical houses and cosy restaurants and keep the water in your eyeline. But while you can get there in one quick drive, it's best to combine it with a trip along the stretch of coastline just outside of Belfast, and add on one of the most famous *Game of Thrones* locations along the way. All in all, it's a great road trip that you can easily tick off in one day – but there are also some lovely places to stay if you want to break it up a little.

Need to Know

Duration: 1 day

Distance: 130km/81 miles

When to go: Early summer, for the Mount Stewart gardens

Start at: Belfast

Finish at: Belfast

The route

Quick view

Crawfordsburn Waterfall.

From **Belfast**, make your way out of the city on the A2 towards **Holywood**, passing Belfast City Airport on the way. If you're staying nearby, there are some excellent restaurants with a neighbourhood vibe in Holywood, like **Noble** and the wine bar **Frae**. Otherwise, continue up along the coast, hopping out along the sea front if you fancy a stroll along the shore.

You'll pass by the **Royal Belfast Golf Club** on your way out to **Helen's Bay**, a worthy detour if you want to see a gorgeous beach. You can walk the couple of miles from Helen's Bay over to **Crawfordsburn Beach** if you'd like, on a lovely coastal trail, but there's a fantastic alternative if you park up in **Crawfordsburn**, where you'll find the **Country Park**. Make your way into the park by way of the **Crawfordsburn Waterfall**, which is right by the village – and if this is as far as you want to go, it's still a lovely stroll into a fairytale woodland thick with ancient, moss-covered trees and a babbling river.

If you fancy a longer walk, head along the riverside trail through the forest all the way to Crawfordsburn Beach. When you're back by the car, there's a charming pub and restaurant called **The Old Inn**, if you're peckish (it's also a great place to stay, if you wanted to start the trip here).

Crawfordsburn Beach.

Back on the road, you'll be turning right on Cootehall Road, aiming for the Crawfordsburn Road that will take you down towards **Strangford Lough**. You'll pass by the **Clandeboye Estate**, a beautiful stretch of land that has another unique accommodation at its heart, **Helen's Tower**. Run by the Irish Landmark Trust, this striking tower was built in 1848 and is one of the most unusual places to stay in Ireland.

You'll pass through **Newtonards** before you hit the water at Strangford Lough. From that point, the road takes you on a waterside journey around the lake, weaving right along the shore. You'll stick to this path all the way to **Mount Stewart**, a grand Neoclassical house now run by the National Trust, with a luxurious home at its core, surrounded by historic gardens and loads of woodland.

The tours of the house are excellent, leading you through the plush rooms filled to the brim with enviable memorabilia – while the Londonderry family still live in the house for half

Helen's Tower, Bangor..

the year, their private rooms are open whenever they're away, so you can nosy around their living room, complete with antiques, oddities and a bar cart fully stocked with champagne, whiskey and gin.

Mount Stewart Boating Lake.

Aerial photo of Portaferry on Strangford Lough.

The gardens have the same touch of eccentricity – keep an eye out for stone statues with names like Charlie the Cheater (Lady Londonderry, who oversaw the interiors and gardens, apparently had a philandering husband). There are some beautiful trails around the estate, where you might spot the native red squirrels, and plenty of knowledgeable gardeners who are happy to chat.

After Mount Stewart, the lake road takes you very briefly inland before leading you back to the water, with old stone walls marking the border. You can keep on that main road from Ardkeen or turn off on the (very narrow) Lough Shore Road to go past Ballyhenry Island, but either one will take you to **Portferry**.

Now, you can either drive about 50 miles around to the village of Strangford, or go for the far more fun option – the ten minute **Strangford Lough Ferry**. Keep an eye on the water as you travel over the mouth of the lough – in 2020, a pod of killer whales was spotted right here.

There are a few spots to wander between in **Strangford** – the excellent seafood restaurant **The Cuan** and the small **Strangford Castle** – but otherwise, head on the Castleward Road to your next destination. Take a right and turn into **Castle Ward**, a vast estate with endless woodland, an eighteenth-century house and a beautiful view down to the lake.

Medieval ruins of Castle Ward.

Landscape of Inch Abbey ruins
in Downpatrick. Co. Down.

But the real appeal is for *Game of Thrones* fans, who'll recognize the estate as the setting for Winterfell. You can download a map to see their shooting locations or find it on site, where you can walk to the place the Stark children practiced archery or where Robert Baratheon made his first appearance.

Make your way back to the road you arrived on, which turns into Strangford Road when you turn right. Follow that winding route through the countryside until you're almost in Downpatrick, where you'll turn right on the Belfast Road to meet **Inch Abbey**, where Robb Stark was proclaimed King of the North in *Game of Thrones*.

Looping back the way you came then up to find the Old Belfast Road, you'll cross the beautiful Quoile Bridge on your way back up to the lake. You'll go right past **Finnebrogue Woods,** where you'll find **Fodder**, an excellent casual restaurant in a giant Nordic teepee, with a roaring fire at its centre. They serve up a lot of fare they grow on site, including beef from their herd of cows, and they sell a lot of produce in their farm shop, too.

You'll then follow the road around the western shore of the lake, though it's not quite as close to the water as the other side, unless you take some of the little detouring roads to and from the lake. One pit stop that's worth the drive is **Tracey's Farmhouse**, which you'll reach after turning right on Ballymorran

Winterfell Tours sign at Castle Ward, a famous filming location for fantasy TV show *Game of Thrones*.

Road. In this traditional farmhouse, you can take workshops in baking, learning how to make things like soda bread and proper scones by the warmth of the fire. That road also leads you back to the water's edge.

Back inland, you'll turn right on Whiterock Road to find Whiterock Bay, and a big local attraction, **Daft Eddy's**. Set on the tiny **Sketrick Island**, you can drive right over the short causeway and up to the bar and restaurant, where they have a lovely outdoor area and a casual menu of light bites for lunch, with local seafood in the evening.

Back on the mainland, follow Ballydorn Road as it loops towards Tullynakil, before finding your way up to **Comber**, a small town with a charming central square. Then it's back up to Newtonards before heading back to Belfast.

Aerial view of Whiterock and Ballydorn bay, with Sketrick Island and Daft Eddy's.

ULSTER – Trip 18: 1 day

Inishowen 100 Coastal Scenic Drive

The largest peninsula in Ireland, Inishowen is also one of the most beautiful. Flung out far on the northernmost tip of the country, this wild and often windswept corner of the land doesn't feel quite as isolated as you may expect – there are biggish towns like Buncrana and villages like Muff along the way, though they are interspersed with empty stretches of coastline, wide beaches and rocky outcrops, the most famous of which is Malin Head, the official end point of the Wild Atlantic Way.

While the Wild Atlantic Way does loop up the western edge of the peninsula, the Inishowen 100 was there first – this coastal lap (named as it's roughly 100 miles long) takes in all of the headland, though it detours down some smaller roads that the Wild Atlantic Way does not. Our road trip is amended slightly too, though for the most part you'll be following the Inishowen 100 route, which is marked with a spiral shape on brown signs. However, we've added a few deviations to bring you to some interesting spots, and this route also starts and ends in Derry, simply because there are more accommodation options. But you can, of course, start wherever you please along the way.

Need to Know

Duration: 1 day

Distance: 200km/124 miles

When to go: March or April, when the roads are quiet

Start at: Derry

Finish at: Derry

Quick view

Day 1: Start off in Derry, heading along the bottom of the Inishowen Peninsula before driving around it in a clockwise direction, past Malin Head and back to your starting point.

Cannon on Derry city walls.

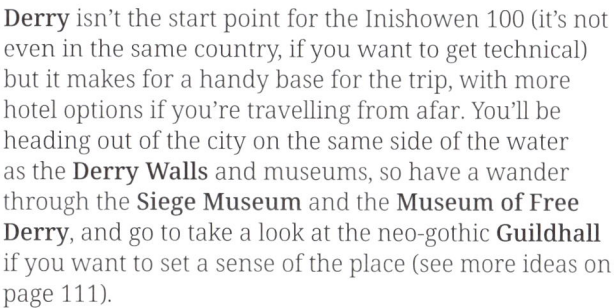

The route

Derry isn't the start point for the Inishowen 100 (it's not even in the same country, if you want to get technical) but it makes for a handy base for the trip, with more hotel options if you're travelling from afar. You'll be heading out of the city on the same side of the water as the **Derry Walls** and museums, so have a wander through the **Siege Museum** and the **Museum of Free Derry**, and go to take a look at the neo-gothic **Guildhall** if you want to set a sense of the place (see more ideas on page 111).

When you're ready to set off, head out in the direction of the Northland Road, turning left onto Buncrana Road towards **Bridgend** and then **Burnfoot**, where you'll meet the Inishowen 100. For the rest of the day, you'll (mostly) be following the brown signs marked 'Inis Eoghain 100' with a spiral shape, which will also mirror the Wild Atlantic Way (the zigzag shapes on a blue background). Keep an eye out for bikes along the way – a lot of people choose to either hike or cycle the full Inishowen 100, and the roads are exceptionally narrow at some stages, with blind bends to contend with as well.

You'll set off on the R238, but if you have an interest in birdlife or want to take a nice hike, take a detour to **Inch Island** (see page 80), which you can drive to on the Inch Road. You could also pay a visit to the **Inch Wildfowl Reserve**, which is on the mainland side.

Aerial view of Buncrana.

Otherwise, stay on track and head along the coastal road by Lough Swilly, passing the first beach you'll spot at **Lisfannon**. There's a huge swathe of wide, sandy beach and thick seagrasses between you and the sea, and there's a Wild Atlantic Way Discovery Point at the other end of the beach.

You'll keep driving up Railway Road (cruelly named for a county with no train lines) and up past the **North West Golf Club**, before heading to **Buncrana**. This is a great spot to get out and stretch the legs, as you can follow the **Buncrana Heritage Walk** to get right out along the water – the full loop is just over two miles, so it doesn't take long. You'll pass by the **Amazing Grace viewing point**, for a lovely look out over the lough, and cross the striking **Castle Bridge** over to the fifteenth-century **O'Doherty's Keep**.

Back in the car, you'll set off further north, turning left on the winding clifftop Fort Dunree Road to the next stop, **Dunree Head**. This globular headland is

everything the Inishowen 100 is about – undulating slopes where slivers of grey rock poke through dense grasses, and craggy edges that jut straight down into the sea.

Pull in and walk first to **Fort Dunree**, an old military fortress perched right on the edge of the clifftop, with great views over the water and of the ragged sheets of rock that lead down to the crystal clear water below. The name in Irish – Dun Fhraoigh – translates to 'Fort of the Heather', and in the summer months the whole headland is bathed in purple as the flowers bloom.

It's now home to an interactive military museum, so you can learn about its history and the coastal landscape, but you can also make use of the walking trails or even go kayaking with **Inish Adventures** in the waters underneath, to view the fort from below. The nearby **Saldanha Suite at Fort Dunree** has more memorabilia, and they also host yoga classes, art exhibitions and have two

Fort Dunree.

virtual reality experiences, too.

When you rejoin the main route, you can turn off to walk the few minutes to **Dunree Bay**, if you want a bit of beach time – this horseshoe curve of bay is protected with sand dunes you walk through to get to the sand.

Back on the road, you'll move inland and then turn right to head up to the **Gap of Mamore**, where the road gets narrower and seems to cut straight through the mountains, those bulbous peaks to either side of the track. It's almost a straight line up to the mountains, with a very, very steep climb (spare a thought for those doing this on two wheels). Keep your wits (and your gear control) about you, as you'll head straight up and over that peak, as the sea stretches out on the horizon.

From there, you'll weave back down, with beautiful views out over the green

Gap of Mamore.

Pollan Bay

fields and down to the water. There's also a small car park if you want to get out and enjoy the views (while giving your nerves a break after driving that hill). There's an exhilarating zigzag in the road almost immediately after, so you'll need to stay alert as you head down.

Soon, you'll find yourself back at sea level, driving through **Ballyliffin**. If you want to see another gorgeous beach, **Pollan Bay**, with a long stretch of sand that overlooks **Malin Head**, the most northerly point in Ireland.

Not too much further on, you can choose to stay on the main route, or take a left to explore the **Isle of Doagh**, to see the sixteenth-century **Carrickabraghy Castle** and the **Doagh Famine Village**, if you're there when it's open in the summer. Here, there are a number of traditional thatched cottages that tell the story of Irish life from the 1840s to present day.

Otherwise, continue to **Carndonagh** and follow the road right back to the water, heading up towards **Malin**. You'll cross the impressive Malin Stone Bridge (which looks better from the water, admittedly) and take a left, driving a curved stretch of road that takes you right alongside the sea and past **Trawbreaga Bay**.

You'll then head up into the hills once more, following a narrow winding path that's surrounded by the bulging globes of the mountain range. The sea comes back into view as the land flattens out again, before you eventually turn left to follow the route up to Malin Head. *Star*

Carrickabraghy Castle.

Wars fans will want to keep an eye out for the road sign on what was the R242, now named the **R2D2** in honour of the scenes shot nearby for *Star Wars: The Last Jedi* – a full scale Millennium Falcon was even built on the clifftops.

You'll drive by the **Malin Head Weather Station**, which fans of the shipping report will appreciate, and follow the road all the way up to Malin Head itself, a dramatic, rugged headland that officially marks the northernmost point on the Irish mainland. There's a small car park, so park up and take a walk along the cliffs to **Hell's Hole**, a subterranean cavern where the sea crashes through, smashing against the triangular rocky peaks that poke out of the water. Whatever you do, take your time exploring (and watch your footing, too).

When you're ready, turn back and drive down the road you came up, stopping if you'd like at **Farrens Bar**, which was a favourite of Mark Hamill's when he was filming *Star Wars*. After that, the route goes inland again, before spitting you out near **Culdaff Beach**, a nice easy strand that's good for swimming.

The next big coastal spot is **Kinnagoe Beach**, considered to be one of the best in Ireland, if not the world – catch it on a sunny day, and it looks like a Caribbean bay, with perfect turquoise water and white sand, surrounded by thickly grass-covered cliffs. It's a very narrow, steep drive to the small car park, but if you fancy your chances of getting a parking space, it's well worth the effort.

Crack on down to the southern coast, passing the Wild Atlantic Way Discovery Point at **Magilligan Point View** for an incredible view out over the coast. If you want to, you can turn left and drive along the coast to walk the trail at the Inishowen Head Loop to see the lighthouse, or you can carry back along the shore road all the way along the southern coast of the peninsula. You'll go past the jagged rocks sticking out of the sands at **Carnagarve Beach**, through **Moville** and **Redcastle** until you reach **Muff**. This is where the Inishowen 100 turns back towards Bridgend, but if you're heading back to Derry you'll stick on the R238 until it turns into the A2 over the border, to drive the final 15 minutes back into the city where you started.

Malin Head.

Leinster – Trip 19: 1 day
Cooley Peninsula

This lesser-trodden corner of the country is an excellent spot for a chilled out drive, where you won't be covering a huge amount of ground but will stop at lovely spots along the way. Bring a bike with you to cycle the Omeath Greenway; pause for a walk on the beach and explore the ancient Hill of Faughart. But whatever you do, be sure to factor in a seafood feast at The Glyde Inn, right on the water's edge with the Cooley Peninsula in the background.

You could also start this route in Dublin, weaving up the north county coast through Rush, Lusk and Skerries. However, that's one of those few routes that's almost better by train, the railway line passing right alongside the shore (and even over the water itself, between Malahide and Donabate). So it's probably better to boot up the M1, and you'll be in Drogheda in less than an hour.

Need to Know

Duration: 1 day

Distance: 148km/92 miles

When to go: Winter, when the roads are quiet

Start at: Drogheda

Finish at: Drogheda

The route

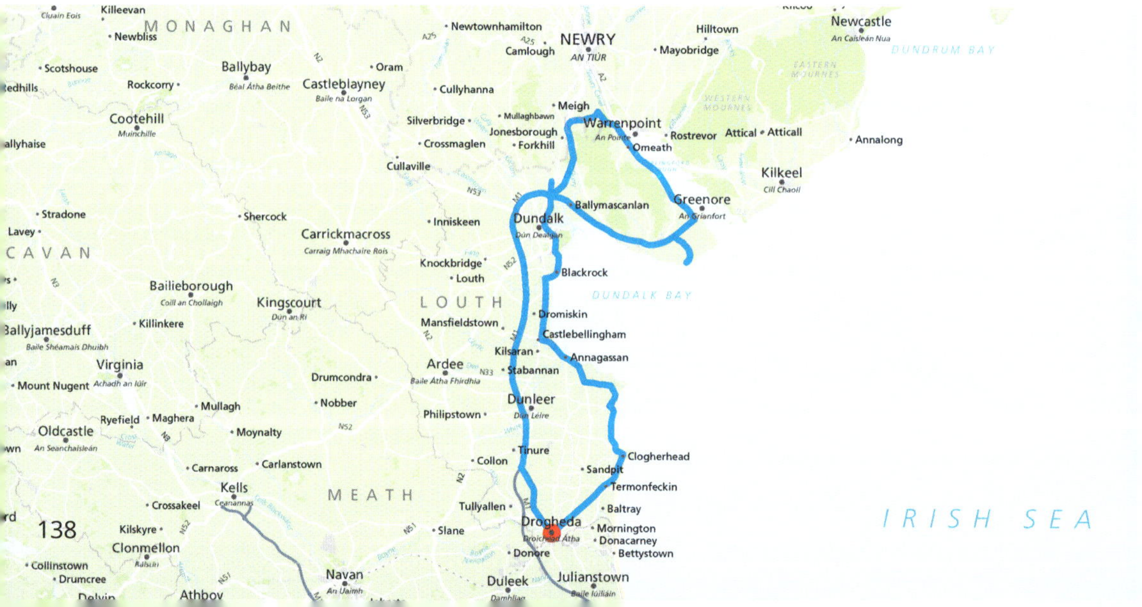

IRISH SEA

Quick view

Day 1: Start off in Drogheda before driving up the Louth coast through Clogherhead and Blackrock, then circumnavigate the Cooley Peninsula before driving back down to Drogheda.

Before you set off from **Drogheda**, take some time to explore the museums that are right in the middle of town. The **Millmount Museum** is set inside a giant Martello tower, which stands on top of a 3,000-year-old mound, which some believe to hold the burial remains of the warrior poet Amergin. Here, you'll find plenty of wartime memorabilia, like muskets used in the Sieges of Drogheda and bayonets from the Battle of the Boyne. There's also a scale model of the Battle of Waterloo, because the Duke of Wellington (who was born in Dublin) has family ties in Drogheda.

Over in the former governor's house, the **Drogheda Museum Millmount** has loads of quirky displays about the local area. There's a room dedicated to eighteenth-century guild and trade banners, spaces replicating traditional homesteads and glass cabinets filled with vintage telephones, retro call cards and a morse code machine. Elsewhere in the courtyard, there are artists' studios where you can buy locally made pieces like knitwear, paintings and silk scarves.

Hugh Delacy Bridge, Drogheda.

In the town itself, you can stroll around **Highlanes Municipal Art Gallery,** where there's a rotating series of contemporary art exhibits. The space itself is beautiful too, with stained glass windows and an excellent café. Drogheda was once a walled city, and just down the road, you can see one of the few parts that's still intact, the thirteenth-century tower of **St Laurence's Gate**. There's a little street food spot just around the corner, too.

Back in the middle of town, **St Peter's Roman Catholic Church** is well worth a visit – it's an impressive building, yes, but it's also the home of the preserved head of Oliver Plunkett. His head was thrown into a fire after he was hung, drawn and quartered in 1681, and later retrieved by his friends – you can still see the burn marks when you peek into the shrine.

Once you're ready to hit the road (and that sight may well make you want to leave town), head out on the R166 towards Termonfeckin, driving to Clogherhead. If you feel like stretching the legs, park up at the **Clogherhead Cliff Walk** just outside of the town. It's a fairly

St Laurence's Gate

short route, following the bumpy trail out along the shore, but you get fantastic views out over the water, with the Mourne Mountains in the distance.

Otherwise, continue up the Coast Road, which passes right alongside the water with some scenic stops along the way – drive up to Dunany Point if you want a nice vantage point. You'll

Clogherhead Cliffs.

Cooley Mountains.

soon be in **Annagassan,** which was the capital of Ireland in Viking times. At **The Glyde Inn,** you can take a virtual reality walk back in time with their Viking VR Experience, where you'll step into the shoes of Bjorn the Bear to see what life was like at this time.

Even if you don't, it's well worth a stop. At the front, The Glyde Inn is every bit the traditional pub, but at the back it opens out to a seafood restaurant set right on the water. The chefs jump over the wall to forage for seaweed and samphire to put on the menu, and the seafood they serve up is as fresh as can be – think slippery razor clams, oysters and giant crab claws. If you'd rather have dinner here at the end of the day, simply drive back down this way instead of the route back down the M1.

Back on the road, you'll pass through **Castlebellingham** and up the Dundalk Road, diverting through **Blackrock** to get the best sea views. You'll bypass Dundalk and then head over the Táin Bridge to

reach the **Cooley Peninsula.** Start off by heading straight over the roundabout to the **Hill of Faughart,** which was the birthplace of St Brigid – they hold a procession here every year on Brigid's Day, and you can visit St Brigid's Well. But it also has fantastic views out over the peninsula, and though it hasn't been excavated, is believed to be a hillfort dating back to the Bronze or Iron Age.

Follow the road you drove up then turn left to drive the southern stretch of the peninsula on the R173. If you didn't eat before, **Carlingford Brewing Company** is a great spot for a wood-fired pizza, or you could turn off just before to head down to **Castlecarragh Bay Beach**. If not, continue to Grange then turn off to drive to **Templetown Beach,** a sheltered bay with excellent rock pooling. With wide sands, it makes for a great walking beach, even in the winter.

Drive back up to meet the road you left, with the mountains rising in the distance, and then turn right to continue on the

King John's Castle, Carlingford.

loop. Turn left onto the R176 and the road will take you right along the edge of **Carlingford Lough,** through the town of **Carlingford** itself. You'll drive past the twelfth-century **Carlingford Castle,** with the mountain of Slieve Foye behind – some say it's the sleeping giant Fionn Mac Cumhaill. You can visit the interior of the castle, which overlooks the harbour.

After this point, the road takes you to **Omeath,** but there's an alternative option – the **Carlingford Lough Greenway.** If you brought the bikes with you, hop out at Carlingford and cycle the almost 7km (4.3 miles) along the coast, for gorgeous views of the water – you'll also stop right by the Hot Box Sauna Carlingford, where you can build up a sweat with a view of the water and the Mourne Mountains.

Back in the car, drive up the R173 in the direction of Newry, but turn off at Ferry Hill to loop off the main route, zip over the border and drive up to the **Flagstaff Viewpoint** in Co Armagh. There, you'll get an incredible view out over the countryside, down the mountains and over to the water. The road up is lovely, too – it's narrow, but

weaves through the forest until you reach the viewpoint, where there's loads of parking.

From there, drive back down into the Republic and you'll pass by the **Ravensdale Forest Recreation Area,** where there are beautiful walking trails including the short Ravensdale loop that'll take you to the ancient standing stones. You can also take a detour here to head to the **Proleek Dolmen,** a megalithic tomb that seems to defy gravity.

When you meet the old roundabout you started the loop on, you can turn right on the M1 to take the quick route back to Drogheda, or follow the same route if you wanted dinner in The Glyde Inn. If you're doing the former, you can take a brief detour to head to **Monasterboices High Cross and Round Tower,** which was founded in the fifth century and has incredibly preserved crosses with historic carvings.

From there, it's just a ten minute drive back into Drogheda.

Monasterboices High Cross and Round Tower.

Flagstaff Viewpoint.

Leinster – Trip 20: 2 days
Boyne Valley Drive

The region of Boyne Valley holds an inordinate number of Ireland's most historic treasures. Within one valley, there are 9,000 years of history, from the Hill of Tara, home to the seat of the High Kings of Ireland, to Newgrange, possibly the most famous passage tomb in the world. The official Boyne Valley Drive is a 225km (140 mile) route that snakes through the countryside of Meath and Louth, calling into the key historical stopping points along the way. It's easy to follow – simply look for the brown signs with a white Celtic spiral shape.

This route largely follows the same pathway, with a few deviations. It's easily customisable – we've split it into a two day trip, overnighting in Kells, but you could also stop in Trim or Athaboy, if that makes more sense. It'll likely be dictated by what time slot you book for Brú na Bóinne, and how long you spend there. Likewise, you don't have to start in Drogheda – you can join the loop at whatever point makes sense for you.

Need to Know

Duration: 2 days

Distance: 180km/112 miles

When to go: April, for longer days but quieter roads

Start at: Drogheda

Finish at: Drogheda

Quick view

Day 1: Drogheda to Kells

Day 2: Kells to Drogheda

Mary McAleese Bridge.

Day 1 – Drogheda to Kells

If you have time to spare in **Drogheda**, see some of the museums and sights in town (see page 139) or, if you're a fan of street art, look up the **DRAWDA Urban Art Trail** and take a self-guided walk around the best murals in town. There are plenty of mythological scenes painted on huge walls, which will get you in the historical spirit for the day ahead.

Your first stop as you head out of the town is the site of the **Battle of the Boyne,** barely a ten-minute drive from Drogheda. If you had the time to spare, you can even walk out to the Battle of the Boyne visitor centre from Drogheda, following the **Boyne greenway** along the edge of the River Boyne – realistically though, this would add half a day to your plans.

The drive is also pretty scenic, taking you right alongside the boardwalk of the greenway and under the Mary McAleese Bridge. You'll continue right along the riverbanks for a peaceful stretch of road that leads you to the main car park, where the visitor centre is a short walk away.

Jan van Huchtenburgh,
A painting of the Battle of the Boyne between the armies of James II and William III, 1690, (detail).

The route

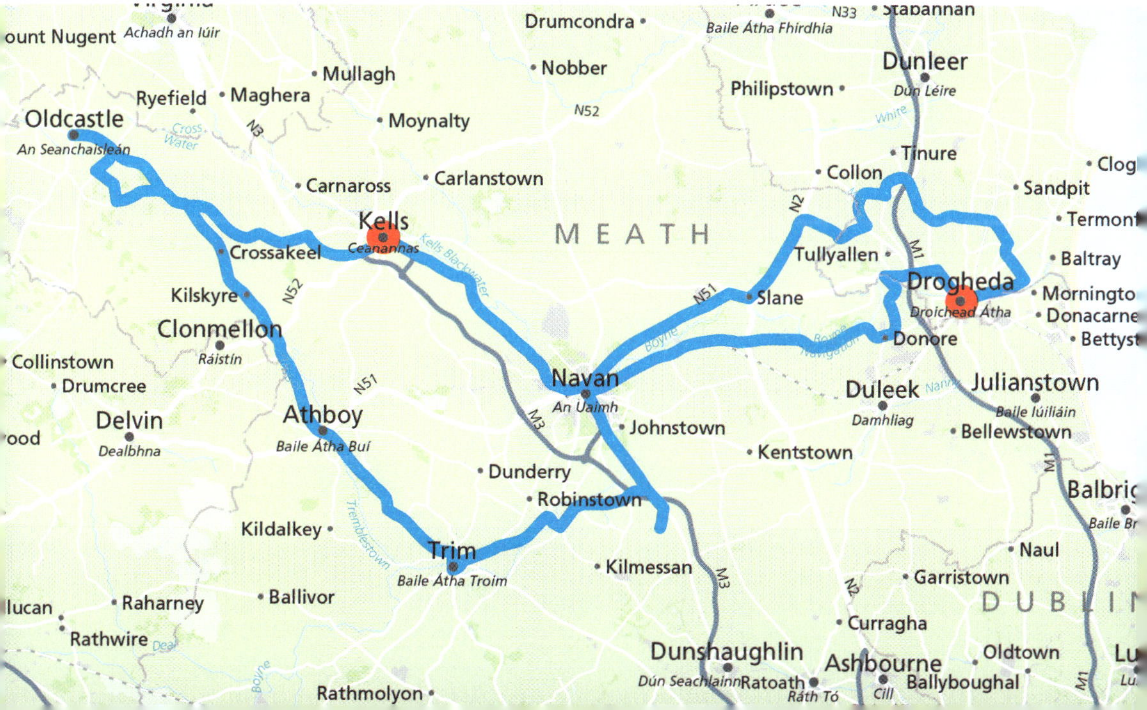

Oldbridge House, Boyne.

The main reception area is in the eighteenth-century **Oldbridge House,** where there's a small exhibition space that'll explain exactly what happened during the Battle of the Boyne. In fact, if you look above the main door at the entrance, you'll see a cannonball that's still wedged in the façade, a visible remnant of the battle itself. There's a visual representation of how the battle unfolded in 1690, with a total of 61,000 men fighting on the fields just in front of the house. Over the courtyard in the old stable there's a cinema room that goes into more detail, and there are also reenactments held throughout the year.

On the grounds, there are some lovely walking trails and an excellent café that overlooks the gardens, which are well worth exploring (the café has a resident cat, too).

You'll follow the long driveway you arrived on to head out to the next stop, **Brú na Bóinne**. Older than both Stonehenge and the Great Pyramids of Giza, the prehistoric passage tombs of Newgrange, Knowth and Dowth make up possibly the most important historical location in Ireland. When you visit, you'll see the largest collection of megalithic art in Western Europe and get to step inside the chamber of a tomb that is bathed in light on just one day a year.

Newgrange stone age passage tomb.

Knowth.

But what's important to know is that you can't just rock up and head inside. You must book your tickets in advance and, crucially, drive to the Brú na Bóinne Visitor Centre and not Newgrange or Knowth, which are listed on maps. The only way to visit either site is on a private minibus that departs from the visitor centre, in order to control traffic and the visitor numbers to both attractions.

Allow a bit of time before your visit though, because the newfangled exhibitions at the visitor centre are top notch, with visual installations, videos explaining the excavation work and plenty of historical information. When your time slot arrives, you'll walk over the bridge to the bus stop and head first to **Knowth**, a passage tomb over 5,000 years old. You're not allowed to access the inside part of the tomb (though you'll likely see rule-breaking rabbits who hop between the grassy domes).

An OPW guide will take you around and show you the megalithic art carved into the rocks outside, where you'll see early lunar depictions that imply a knowledge of the ancient calendar. You're also able to walk up the steps and on to the very top of the dome, with great views of the nearby historic sights – you can see the **Hill of Slane** and **Newgrange**, too.

Afterwards, you'll be driven to Newgrange and wait your turn to enter the chamber. Inside, they reenact the moment the sun rises at the winter solstice, for which this tomb is famous. On that day, the sun aligns with the entrance of the passage tomb and bathes the whole chamber in light. You'd have to be incredibly lucky to see the sight itself (there's a free lottery each year) but when the guide switches off the lights and the replica beam appears, you get a fair idea of how that magical moment would feel.

When you're finished and dropped off back at the visitor centre, you'll head into **Navan** and then out to the next stop, the **Hill of Tara**. There was a passage tomb

Hill of Tara.

built here in the Stone Age, but it became more important later as the seat of the High Kings of Ireland. All of the old roads in Ireland lead to the Hill of Tara, and it's accessible all year round, though the visitor centre is only open from May to September.

Next up is **Bective Abbey,** a beautiful twelfth-century Cistercian abbey featuring remarkable cloisters within. You'll then loosely follow the path of the River Boyne until you reach **Trim** and its castle, the largest Anglo-Norman fortification in Ireland. A guided tour of this castle is fascinating, taking you up to the top for views out over the surrounding hills and fields. It's not just one for history buffs, either – it was a major filming location for *Braveheart*, so there are plenty of movie stories too.

The next town you'll hit is **Athaboy**, and you can take a detour here if you want to see the prehistoric **Hill of Ward**. Otherwise, crack on in the direction of

Trim Castle.

Loughcrew Cairns Historic Passage Tomb Relic.

Loughcrew, where you'll drive a bit of a loop to see the **Loughcrew Megalithic Cemetery**. This collection of Neolithic passage tombs is spread out over four sloping hills, and date back to 3000 BC. You can explore this site alone, but it's best to take one of the free tours that are available from June to September.

Afterwards, you can explore the extensive gardens and grounds of **Loughcrew Estate**, where there's a medieval motte and Saint Oliver Plunkett's church – his family lived on the estate before Oliver Cromwell stole it in 1641.

Then it's a short drive to **Kells**, where you'll stay for the night – the Headfort Arms Hotel is a lovely option.

Day 2 – Kells to Drogheda

Spend the morning seeing a little of Kells, wandering around the old abbey where the Book of Kells was kept hidden from Vikings. You can also see the round tower on the same Kells Monastic Site, though only from the outside – if you want to climb a tower, you can head to the Spire of Lloyd a short distance outside of Kells.

From the top, you have great views out over the countryside.

Head out of Kells on the R163, crossing the handsome stone **Headfort Bridge** and driving through the countryside until you meet Slane. One of the biggest attractions here is **Slane Castle**, the grounds of which have seen many a large-scale concert – the Rolling Stones, Bob Dylan and Bruce Springsteen have all played here.

Unfortunately, they no longer offer regular castle tours, unless you're there for afternoon tea on set dates. It's worth keeping an eye on their calendar though, as they're open during Heritage Week

Book of Kells.

and for certain markets. What is open for tours is their distillery, right next door. It's an interesting walk through their history and the story of their whiskey, culminating in a tasting for the non-drivers.

In the village of Slane, there are some quaint bakeries and cosy pubs where you can grab a bite to eat. Just outside the village, you can park up to walk to the **Hill of Slane**, where St Patrick lit the Paschal fire in the year 433 and changed the course of Irish history. You can walk around the remains of **Slane Abbey**, between elaborately carved Celtic crosses, graves and a tribute to St Patrick, and you can also go inside what was built as a college for priests. You can even climb the crooked old stone steps inside, for an even better view out over the Boyne Valley.

From here, you'll deviate from the official Boyne Valley Drive somewhat and keep heading up the N2, which brought you to the Hill of Slane. Turn right on the L5605 then right again at Melifont at the Louth border. **Old Mellifont Abbey** was the first Cistercian monastery in Ireland, created in 1142, and is still an architectural marvel to this day. Though it's more ruin in some places, you can still see grand archways, pillars and the two-storey octagonal lavabo.

Less than ten minutes away, you can see another historic gem, the **Monasterboices High Cross and Round Tower** (see page 143). You can drive the quick way back to Drogheda from here, but if you have an interest in more recent history then loop around the other side of the city to see Beaulieu House, a seventeenth-century private home that's open for tours in the summer months. It's set right on the banks of the River Boyne, which makes the drive back into Drogheda particularly special, hugging the edge of the water (though granted, it gets far less scenic when you pass the manufacturing plants).

Slane Abbey.

Old Mellifont Abbey.

Leinster – Trip 21: 3 days
Ireland's Ancient East

Take a few days to explore the region known as Ireland's Ancient East, and you'll come across scenic beaches, mountain ranges and historic country homes. The eastern coast is also scattered with some of Ireland's most appealing towns and cities, so you can intersperse the natural beauty with some exploration of places like Waterford and Wexford, before heading inland to Kilkenny and Kildare. There's a huge scope of attractions in this corner of the country, and our itinerary packs a lot in, so you can pick and choose what takes your interest. This three-day trip cherry picks some of the highlights of the region, but you don't need to stop at every single location – unless you want to, of course.

Need to Know

Duration: 3 days

Distance: 512km/318 miles

When to go: May, when the smaller attractions reopen for the season

Start at: Dublin

Finish at: Dublin

The route

Quick view

Day 1: Set off from Dublin along the coast to Wicklow, stopping at Powerscourt before finishing up in Wexford

Day 2: Leave Wexford and drive to Kilkenny, via Waterford and Tipperary

Day 3: Check out some historical houses on the way from Kilkenny to Dublin

Day 1 – Dublin to Wexford

Start off your trip in **Dublin,** starting with a bit of time in the city without using the car. It's best not to drive through the city centre if you can help it – if you're visiting from elsewhere, pick a hotel near an exit point so you can avoid as much of the traffic as possible. For this route, a good option is Haddington House in Dún Laoghaire, which will skip the busiest parts of town. Or the InterContinental in Ballsbridge, where it'll be easier to set off.

When you're in the city, there are plenty of places that are a little more off the tourist track, or good options if you feel like you know all of the main attractions. While the Long Room in Trinity College is a must, as is their new Book of Kells exhibition, Marsh's Library is a beautiful space that's barely changed in the past 300 years. If you're starting outside of the city centre, there's a lovely walk that goes from Sandymount all the way along the shoreline towards the Bull Wall, where you can walk the length of the old stone to the bright red lighthouse at the end.

When you're ready to hit the road, make your way out of town to the coast at **Sandymount.** There are some good coffee shops in the village, so you can grab some caffeine and a pastry before you set off. Then drive down the coast road, with Dublin Bay to your left. You'll

Trinity College.

The Forty Foot, Dun Laoghaire.

pass through **Blackrock, Seapoint** and **Monkstown**, driving by the neat rows of white townhouses that line the coast, before reaching **Dún Laoghaire.**

If you want to explore a little, park up and walk around the harbour and People's Park, where there's a food market every Sunday. If you want more of a stroll, walk out the length of the East Pier, being sure to kick the lighthouse wall at the end (otherwise it doesn't count). If you're a sea swimmer, you'll want to join the throngs of people who take a dip at the **Forty Foot** every single day, no matter what the weather is doing – you can park up nearby, but it's nicer to walk along the coast and not worry about securing a spot.

If you have the time, pop into the tiny **James Joyce Museum** located in the Martello tower where he briefly lived (and where he set the opening scenes of Ulysses, where the character of Buck Mulligan also took a dip in the 'snot green' 'scrotum-tightening sea' at the Forty Foot).

Otherwise, keep driving south through **Dalkey**, home of Bono and some of Dublin's priciest real estate. It's a narrow enough route, but a drive down the **Vico Road** is well worth it – the view out over the bay is incredible, well earning the nickname of Dublin's Bay of Naples. Hop out at **Killiney** if you fancy a walk on the beach or a session in the Hot Box Sauna, then make your way down towards Shankhill and say goodbye to the narrow roads.

You'll soon pass over the border into the greenery of County Wicklow, passing pretty cottages until you reach **Enniskerry**. There's more than a little dash of the fairytale aesthetic to this village, so it makes sense that the Disney movie Disenchanted was filmed here. Nowadays, it's a pretty spot to walk around, with a handsome town triangle and charming cottages.

Just outside the village, you'll turn onto the Eagle Valley to head towards the **Powerscourt Estate** – stop first at the Sugar Loaf Viewpoint for a great vantage point of Wicklow's iconic mountain. There's plenty to see at Powerscourt, with 47 acres of immaculate gardens, a whiskey distillery and the grand house itself, a Palladian mansion that dates back to 1741 and stands overlooking the estate.

There are some lovely shops inside the house, as well as the Avoca terrace café, so you can sit outside with a pot of tea and a slice of cake. Be sure to spend enough time exploring the gardens, because there's a lot to see – highlights are the Italian garden with staggered terraces leading down to the lake and a view of the Sugar Loaf, and the pet cemetery.

The nearby Powerscourt Waterfall is technically part of the estate but does require an additional ticket – it's worth the fee though, particularly after a period of heavy rain. The cascades power over 121 metres (397 feet) of rock, making it Ireland's highest waterfall.

When you're ready to go, head back towards the N11 via Kilmaacanoge, calling into the big Avoca there if you need to pick up any picnic bits for the next few days. There are a few little detours you can make if you please – stopping into Greystones or Delgany (there is a great drive-thru coffee stand there, The Fat Fox, if you're in need).

But otherwise, you're simply driving through the Garden of Ireland, turning off on the L1113 to see a place even more deserving of the name, the **National Botanic Gardens** at Kilmanogue. They're

Powerscourt Estate, Wicklow.

particularly beautiful in April, when the extensive collection of rhododendrons bloom in a spectacular display of colour.

Back on the road, your next stop is **Avondale House,** where you'll find both the eighteenth-century home that was once inhabited by Samuel Hayes and the Parnell Family, and the treetop walk, **Beyond the Trees.** This raised walkway weaves through the treetops, ending at a viewing tower 38 metres off the ground – if you can buy an additional ticket, you can even slide down to the bottom.

From there, you'll sweep down back in the direction of the coast, sticking on the M11 past Arklow and Gorey until you reach **Wexford,** your home for the night.

Day 2 – Kilkenny to Dublin

On your way out of Wexford, you'll pass by the **Irish National Heritage Park** at Ferrycarrig, a great outdoor museum that covers 9,000 years of Irish history. You can check out a Stone Age settlement, a Viking set up and see what early Christian life was like in Ireland – you can even do that dressed like a Viking, if that's your cup of tea.

You'll drive briefly along the edge of the River Slaney before turning off to meet the N25 to get to **New Ross**. Skirt your way around the city to find the River Barrow and stop at the **Dunbrody Famine Ship Experience,** moored right on the water. This ship is an authentic replication of a vessel that sailed in the 1840s, and tells the story of those forced to emigrate during the Great Famine.

Walk of Beyond the Trees, Wicklow.

Irish National Heritage Park.

When you cross the river, you'll pass briefly into County Kilkenny, driving down through the countryside until you arrive into **Waterford**, Ireland's oldest city. If you're a museum nut, you have a good few to choose from – there are five experiences that make up **Waterford Treasures.** There's the Medieval Museum, which incorporates the thirteenth-century Choristers' Hall and the fifteenth-century Mayor's Wine Vault, the Irish Silver Museum, the Irish Museum of Time and the Irish Wake Museum, which covers the rituals of death. There's also Bishop's Palace, where you can take a Bridgerton-esque tour of the grand Georgian mansion and see the world's oldest surviving piece of Waterford glass.

On that note, the **House of Waterford** crystal is right in the middle of the town, too. Out on the other side of town, you'll pass by Mount Congreve House and Gardens, home to one of the world's largest private collection of plants. As well as the extensive gardens, you can

Dunbrody Famine Ship.

have lunch in the Stables Café or spend the night in one of their forest cabins or gate lodges.

When you're ready to depart, set off for Tipperary and the pretty town of **Carrick-on-Suir,** which is a nice spot to stretch the legs if you feel like it. Otherwise, head on up on the N76 towards **Kilkenny**.

How much you see here depends on how your day panned out, so if you don't get to see any of the sight tonight you can at least enjoy a nice meal and a pint in one of the town's restaurants or pubs – try the Michelin-starred Campagne, or Petronella.

Day 3 – Kilkenny to Dublin

Start off your day with a tour of **Kilkenny Castle,** or at the very least a walk around its beautiful grounds. This thirteenth-century castle is right in the middle of the town, and was the home of the Butlers of Ormonde for over 600 years. Now, it's been carefully refurbished to look as it would have done in the 1830s.

Afterwards, head to the **Medieval Mile** – you can visit the Medieval Mile Museum, or pop into Rothe House, a sixteenth-century merchant house with an excellent gift shop. If you have a bit more time to spare, there are some great walking tours of the city – Shenanigans cover all the historic sights in 90 minutes, and the guides are upbeat and fun.

When you're ready to depart, head out of town on the N78, then the N80, making your way through Stradbally (the home of the Electric Picnic) and then to the **Rock of Dunamase.** This Celtic fortification looks a little reminiscent of the Rock of Cashel, with fragments of the fortress standing on a grassy knoll overlooking the countryside.

From there, you'll skirt around the edge of Portlaoise, then head up on the M7. If you want to, you can detour to go to **Emo Court and Parklands** in the Slieve Blooms, with giant Sequoia trees in the expansive gardens, lakeside trails and a tearoom that's open every day apart from Christmas.

The River Suir at Carrick-on-Suir.

The Rock of Dunamase.

Back on the road, you'll drive on the not very exciting M7 into Kildare, passing by Kildare Village and heading to the **National Stud and Gardens.** Depending on where your interests lie, you'll either call into the Irish Racehorse Experience, to find out about the local connections to racing, or the beautiful Japanese Gardens, designed in the early 1900s to emulate the space you might see in Japan, with ornate bridges, ponds and rocks.

From there, you'll loop up through Kildare until you reach Celbridge and Castletown House, a Palladian mansion that was built in the 1720s. The grounds are exceptional, with over 200 acres of woodland to explore.

When you leave, the drive back to Dublin is about 30 minutes, and you'll be right back where you started.

Japanese garden at the Irish National Stud.

LEINSTER – Trip 22: 1 day

Wicklow Mountains and Glendalough

Need to Know

Duration: 1 day

Distance: 130km/81 miles

When to go: April or May, when the days are longer but the crowds haven't yet formed

Start at: Dublin

Finish at: Dublin

You can't talk about road trips without mentioning Wicklow. A day spent pootling around the mountains, weaving around the roads that wind around the foothills and lead you up and over the peaks, is one of the best days you could spend behind the wheel. It's amazing if you're a hiker, but you can also just stay in the car for the day, checking out the mountain scenery through the windscreen (also handy if the weather turns, as is its wont). History fans will also be kept happy with the monastic sites and historic houses, and there are some excellent places to eat along the way, too. This trip packs a lot into the day, so allow a bit of extra time if you're hiking. It's worth noting that this region can get exceptionally busy, both with road trippers and tourist coaches, so avoid summer weekends if you can, particularly if you are including a stop in Glendalough.

The route

Quick view

Day 1: Start off in Dublin, checking out the mountains on the way out to Wicklow, where you'll tick off the national park, Sally Gap and Glendalough.

Snow on a waterfall in the Glencree River.

Dublin Mountains.

Make your way out of **Dublin** (if that's where you're starting from) and depart the city on the R115, in the direction of the **Dublin Mountains** – this turns into Military Road the further up you get. If you want to start the day with a quick hike, call into the **Hell Fire Club**, which you'll drive right past.

Once an eighteenth-century gentleman's club, this now abandoned lodge is somewhat creepy (and haunted, depending on who you believe) but while the shell of the building is cool to see, you're here more for the views over Dublin. You'll look out over the city, out to the sea and down to the Wicklow Mountains, too.

Back on the road, you'll carry on through the mountains and the pine tree forests (pausing at the Killakee View Point, if you fancy it) until you skirt over the border into Wicklow. The fields to the side of the road are thick with heather and fern, with the odd remnant of old stone walls poking through greenery. The road gets narrow and windy here, and you can stop quickly to see the waterfall at Glencree if you'd like. You'll also pass by Lough Bray, where there's a walking loop to see the lake – it has a fair elevation gain though, and it's almost 7km long.

The road takes you up and over the peaks, until you're in the **Wicklow Mountains National Park**. You're now approaching one of the most beautiful drives in the country – turn right onto the R759 and you'll be at the **Sally Gap**. It's narrow enough, but there's good visibility and a few lay byes where you can pull in to let someone else pass. The views are exceptional, with the mountains in the background and picture-perfect swathes of green in front – it's quintessential Wicklow.

The road snakes down, over the Cloghoge River and the Ballysmuttan Bridge that would, to most people, just be a pretty spot – the river slices through the undulating mountain with boulders peppered in the water. But for some, it's known as something else – the *PS I Love You* **Bridge,** where the two characters met in the movie of the same name.

Pretty soon after, you'll get your first glimpse of **Lough Tay**, known to most as the Guinness Lake, due to its dark, inky colour. It's a spectacular sight, and as you get closer the road takes you through the forest, which clears to bring you to the viewpoint for a cracking view out down and over the water. But the views are just as good as you carry on the road, the single lane track standing high over the water to your right. There are a few places to park when the road opens out, if you want to hike up one of the trails to see the lake from slightly higher.

You can also stop at **Ballinastoe Woods** to walk along those trails, if you'd rather a stomp through the trees. Otherwise, the drive takes you through the forestry, until you come down and turn right into Roundwood. This is a good stopping point for lunch, with several cosy pubs where you can tuck into some comfort food by a roaring fire. Try The Roundwood Inn, The Coach House or Roundwood Stores, a more casual set up where you can get towering focaccia sandwiches and

The *PS I Love You* bridge.

excellent coffee. If you did fancy a walk here, you can head off around the **Vartry Reservoir**, the trail dipping between the woodland and around the edge of the water.

Vartry Reservoir.

When you're ready, head out on the R755 and drive through the trees and past the fancy houses to your next stop, **Glendalough**. Call in first to the visitor centre and see how busy it is – it may be easier to park here and walk, but if not there's a car park at Glendalough Upper. Either way, you'll want to stop here first, as it's the access point for the **Glendalough Monastic Site.**

The site dates back to the sixth-century, and you'll find a remarkably intact collection, including the round tower, stone churches and ornately carved crosses. You can learn all about it in the visitor centre before wandering around to take it all in yourself.

If you're up to it, it's definitely worth doing one of the walking trails around Glendalough itself. There are nine

different paths, from the 1.6km route up to see **Poulanass waterfall,** to a hefty 11km climb up the Spinc. The 3km Miners' Road Walk is a lovely path along the water's edge, but there's a good variety in the rest – you can see all the trail info at the National Park Visitor Centre.

Be warned, this is the area that can get dense with traffic, particularly during a summer weekend. If you want to make this a priority, arrive early – particularly if you want to climb the Spinc.

When you're ready, head back to meet the same road you arrived on and continue on the R756, driving through this stunning glacial valley. If you want to see St Kevin's Pool, you can park up right at the roadside and walk the ten minutes down to the mythical body of water, said to be where the saint bathed

Glendalough Monastic Site.

Phoenix Park.

and meditated (it's freezing, if you want to give it a go yourself).

You'll pass over another bridge, and from there continue to soak in the pretty countryside. Turn right onto the R758 and you'll soon be in **Blessington**, the road passing around the edge of the lake with the same name. Cross over the River Liffey and head out of the town to **June Blake's Garden,** an immaculate 3-acre garden you can tour in the summer. They sometimes run events here, too.

Back on the road, you'll follow the N81 back into County Dublin, making your way back into the city however the traffic dictates. But if you do fancy tacking on another great outdoor space, stop off at the **Phoenix Park** on your way home. The largest enclosed city park in Europe and home to both the president, the US ambassador and a huge herd of fallow deer, the Phoenix Park is a beautiful space.

If you arrive at dusk and drive up the main throughfare, Chesterfield Avenue, you'll see the Victorian gas lamps that line the road flicker into life, casting a dim pool of amber light on the pathways below. They're still tended to by hand, by the same family who've maintained and minded them since 1890. They're some of the last of their kind in Europe, and make for a beautiful sight at the light fades.

Phoenix Park gas lamps.

Blessington Lake.

LEINSTER – Trip 23: 1 day

Slieve Bloom Mountains Scenic Drive

The Slieve Bloom Mountains are something of an open secret in Ireland – the area definitely doesn't have the same footfall that Wicklow or Kerry would get, but this relatively small pocket of land has some of the finest scenery around. Linking Laois and Offaly, these gently rolling mountains are some of the oldest in Europe, and if you get to a high point on a clear day it's said you can see the high points of all four of the ancient Irish provinces. It's also a walker's paradise – there are plenty of beautiful trails that weave through woodlands and up mountains, and there's even an annual Slieve Blooms Walking Festival, usually held on the May bank holiday.

There are three official Slieve Bloom Scenic Drives, and this route loosely links two of them, the Village and Heritage Driving Route and the Glendine Driving Route. Some of the sections are signposted like the Wild Atlantic Way or Inishowen 100, but even if not, the roads are easy to follow – if rather narrow in places.

Need to Know

Duration: 1 day

Distance: 138km/86 miles

When to go: May

Start at: Kinnitty

Finish at: Kinnitty

Quick view

Day 1: Head off from Kinnitty, driving in two loops around the Slieve Bloom Mountains to explore the walking trails and take in the views.

Birr Castle.

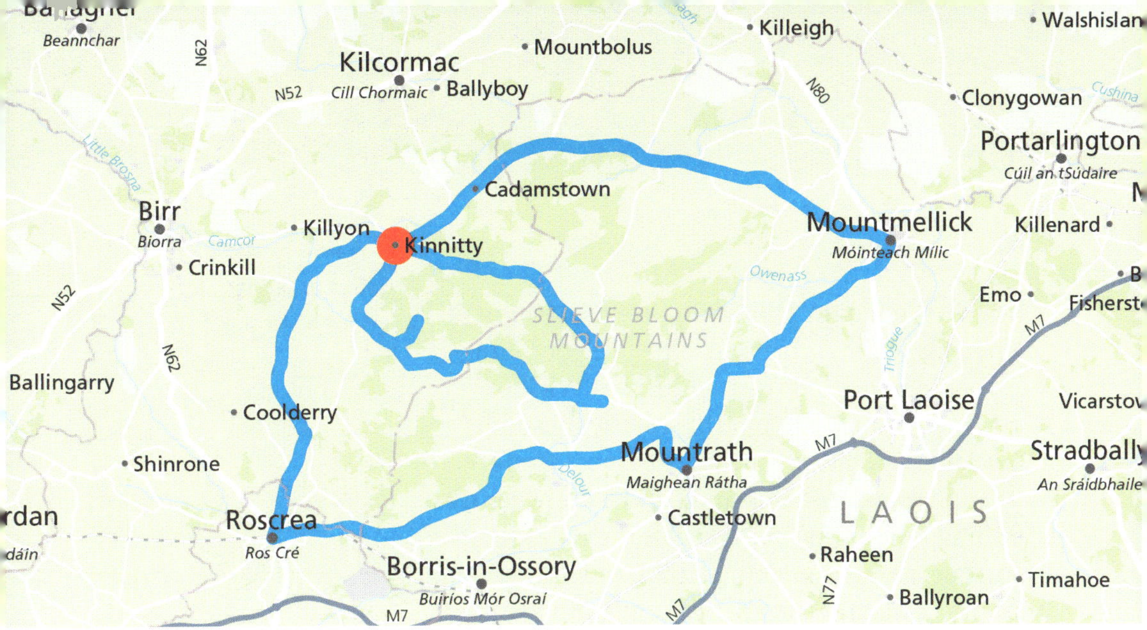

Start off in the pretty village of **Kinnitty,** which is also (and perhaps oddly) home to a pyramid built in the early 1800s and inspired by the Great Pyramid of Giza in Egypt. It was built by (and now holds the remains of) the Bernard family who owned Kinnitty Castle, now a hotel that's a great place to stay. You can also stay in the nearby Birr, where you can visit the Birr Castle Demesne and Historic Science Centre – they run tours of the castle in the summer months, and there's 120 acres of parkland to explore.

When you're ready to start the drive, head south on the Ballyshane Road, following the quiet route through the countryside. Turn left on the Tulla and Crumlin road to follow the narrow country boreen to **Glenafelly Forest Recreation Area**, one of the most remote parts of the Slieve Blooms. This is more for those who want to hike – if that's not your thing, stick to the road you were on. But if you do, allow a couple of hours to hike the 7km Glenafelly Eco Walk, which will take you through the ancient woodland.

Back on the road, you'll drive along Ballynalack, a narrow road surrounded by thick trees, until it opens up to reveal the meadows and meandering slopes of the mountains. Keep an eye on your speed and go as slowly as you can, because there's a sharp hairpin turn

Leap Castle.

coming up, as the road snakes through the forests once more. As the road rises, the views of the mountains get better and better. There are some more hairpin turns coming, until the road spits you out near **Lissenhall,** where you'll turn left on to the L1031. You'll pass by the River Delour Picnic Area, handy if you have lunch with you, then carry on to **Lacca Wood**, home to some pretty trails, and the nearby Lacca Church, if you want to see either of those.

Otherwise, it's back on the L1030 up to Killanure, turning left on the R440 and following the gently curved route all the way to **Gorteenameala Eco Trail**. It's an easy enough linear trail, so you can just walk a stretch of it and turn back whenever you please. It's a good option if you want a quick stretch of the legs.

When you're back on the R440, you'll head up and over the mountains for a gorgeous stretch of road that leads you all the way back to Kinnitty, the Slieve

Bloom Mountains either side of you. You'll once again pass through the dense forestry and greenery, before you're back in the village, where you'll head straight through on the same road (stopping for a spot of lunch if you're hungry).

Now, you're on the Village and Heritage driving route. Head straight out of Kinnitty on the R440, then turn left on the R421 through Clareen. Soon, you'll drive right by **Leap Castle,** supposedly the most haunted castle in the world. It's a private home but open for visitors, though you may want to call ahead, to make sure they're open. There, you can hear stories of the bloody battles and history over the centuries, and the ghoulish sightings that the family who live there now have seen.

From there, you'll carry on the quiet country road, nipping over the border into Tipperary to stop at **Roscrea** to see **Roscrea Castle, Gardens** and **Damer House**, and the **Black Mills**. Open from

March to October, there's a stone motte castle that dates back to the 1280s, as well as a beautiful pre-Palladian architecture house from the eighteenth-century. You can head inside the Damer House and also walk through the extensive gardens.

Heading back into Offaly, you'll find the R445 and rejoin the loop, turning left on the L1050 – if you want to see another historic property, Ballaghmore Castle is just off the road, though it's most commonly rented privately. Follow this road up through the hills and you'll reach **Poet's Cottage**, a replica thatched cottage that shows you what life would have looked like in rural Ireland in the 1800s. Inside, however, it's a more contemporary community café, where you can get a coffee and a sausage roll for the road.

Soon you'll be in **Mountrath,** where you'll follow the road out to **Ballyfin,** one of Ireland's most luxurious hotels. This neoclassical mansion was finished in 1826 and has been a private family home, then a boarding school, before becoming the lavish property it is today. If you're not staying (and if you are, it's the ultimate treat) you can book dinner in the Michelin-starred restaurant, but otherwise you'll continue on to Mountmellick.

From there, take the R422 through the Laois countryside. If you have it in you to do another walk, then stop at the **Brittas Forest Recreation Area** and do the 6km loop out to see Brittas Lake (or you can drive back here on another day instead, it's a 15 minute drive from Kinnitty).

Otherwise, the road takes you right back to your start point, and your double loop is complete.

Roscrea and Roscrea Castle.

LEINSTER – Trip 24: 2 days

Ireland's Hidden Heartlands

The west coast has the Wild Atlantic Way. The other side has Ireland's Ancient East. So what to do with the middle? The answer is Ireland's Hidden Heartlands, a catch-all term for the central-ish part of the country, made up of Leitrim, Cavan, Roscommon, Westmeath and Offaly, with a little bit of Tipperary thrown in for good measure – Fermanagh was just recently added to the mix, too.

But this road trip focuses on one core area, heading from Athlone up into Leitrim through Roscommon, in a central zone that encompasses sixth-century monastic sites, meandering waterways and grand country houses. You could easily link this one up with the Leitrim and Roscommon road trip on page 38, if you wanted a three-day trip, or mix and match the itineraries, using Carrick-on-Shannon as a base.

Much like the spirit of the region, this is a laid-back road trip where you'll drift through the countryside, past lakes and distant mountain ranges, hopping out of the car when you spot a nice picnic area or lakeside bench. And it's a good idea to pack a picnic for this one – when you're in the depths of the countryside, a great place to eat isn't always guaranteed, so shop in advance to avoid disappointment at lunchtime.

Need to Know

Duration: 2 days

Distance: 291km/180 miles

When to go: June, when more places are open for the season

Start at: Athlone

Finish at: Athlone

Quick view

Day 1: Head off from Athlone and drive first to Clonmacnoise, before heading back up north and skirting by Lough Ree up into Carrick-on-Shannon.

Day 2: Leave Carrick-on-Shannon and explore Roscommon, looping down the other side of the lake to end up back in Athlone.

The route

Athlone Castle.

Day 1 – Athlone to Carrick-on-Shannon

Athlone is a charming town with plenty of history – you've probably got time for one sight this morning, but it's better to allow a full day before the road trip to explore. **Athlone Castle** is right at the heart of it all, a twelfth-century fortress that has seen many a battle over the centuries, as well as an incident where a freak lightning strike blew up 260 barrels of gunpowder and thousands of grenades.

Inside, there are immersive exhibitions, like the one telling the story of the Great Siege of Athlone, and you can climb up the defensive walls for a great view out over the river and the town – there's also a giant chess board there if you fancy a game. **Luan Gallery** is just over the road and great for a spot of artsy culture, and there are some good places to pick up a picnic – try Bastion Foods for sandwiches and wraps.

The first spot on today's itinerary can be reached by car, but if you wanted to, you could always catch the boat from Athlone, the journey taking about 90 minutes and sailing all the way down the River Shannon until you're at **Clonmacnoise.**

Clonmacnoise Monastic Site.

But while the river is more scenic, the drive takes less than half an hour. You'll aim for the N62, turning onto the L3008 and driving to the end of the R444, where you'll see the River Shannon and the first glimpse of ancient ruins. **Clonmacnoise Monastic Site** was founded in the sixth century, and was once a university where students came from all over Europe to study. Now, you'll find a smattering of structures on the banks of the river, including a cathedral, two round towers, nine churches and hundreds of Early Christian grave slabs.

There's an audiovisual presentation inside where you can learn all about the history, and see some of the original high crosses that are kept inside for preservation (the ones outside are replicas).

When you're ready to go, head back towards Athlone but take a right onto the R916 to meet the N62, to drive along the dense countryside that lines the shores of **Lough Ree**. If you want a quicker drive,

Lough Ree.

Portlick Millennium Forest.

you can stick to the N55, but if you like a bit of waterside distraction then head into **Wineport Lodge**. There's beautiful accommodation here, but it's also a fantastic spot to stop for lunch, right on the water (they also have floating hot tubs, if you're staying the night).

Even if you're not stopping, it's a lovely riverside road to drive, and it'll lead you to the pretty village of **Glasson**. Again, you can shoot on the N55 but it's worth driving the Benown road out towards Portlick (just beware, the road is fairly narrow and people can drive at a fair clip along it). You could skirt off to Glasson Lakehouse, another lovely waterside spot for lunch or a night's sleep, but otherwise head straight to **Portlick Millennium Forest.**

There are beautiful walking trails here and they're not too long, either – most take you through the mossy woodlands to the lakeshore, for stunning views of Lough Ree. You can loop the whole thing (there's a trail guide at the car park) but you can also walk out to the water and as far along as you please, before heading back to the car. If you did bring a picnic, this is the place for it.

You can take the winding country roads or you can nip along the N55, which will speed you up towards Ballymahon. Instead, turn left onto the L1131 to drive through the Longford countryside – you can also dip out onto the lake here for some viewpoints or to see the harbours where the boats park up as they manoeuvre along the Shannon.

Roscommon Castle.

When you get up to Lanesborough, you'll cross the bridge and move over into County Roscommon, following the N63 all the way to **Roscommon** town. Here, you can park up and visit **Roscommon Castle,** which is open for weekend tours during the summer. Alternatively, take a walk through **Loughnaneane Park** where you'll get beautiful views of the castle's exterior from the pond.

Your next spot is a short drive away in **Strokestown**. **The National Famine Museum** in **Strokestown Park** has recently had a big overhaul and was redeveloped to include a more immersive, interactive experience, and you'll get to see the vast difference between the life of an aristocratic landlord and their tenants during the famine. There are touchscreens and

audio for a self-guided tour, and many of the stories come from the meticulous notes made by the former owner of Strokestown Park, Major Denis Mahon, who was the first landlord to be assassinated during the famine.

You can also take a guided tour of **Strokestown Park House,** and it's well worth taking a bit of time to explore the grounds, too – the Victorian rose garden is lovely, particularly when the flowers are in bloom.

From there, **Carrick-on-Shannon** is about a 30-minute drive away, and your stopping point for the night. See page 38 if you need any ideas, and if you're looking for a nice dinner spot then head to The Oarsman, one of the longest-running gastropubs around.

Boyle Cistercian Abbey.

Day 2 – Carrick-on-Shannon to Athlone

Set off from Carrick-on-Shannon on the N4, stopping first at **Lough Key Forest Park** (see page 39), for a stroll through the woodlands and out onto the lake, which is worth it for the magical glimpse of McDermott Castle on a tiny lake isle.

From there, it's a quick drive to **Boyle**, where you can call into **Boyle Cistercian Abbey,** built by monks from **Mellifont Abbey** (see page 150). It was decimated by Cromwellian forces and later battles, but what remains is beautiful, and it's open for visitors from March to September. There's an information point in a gatehouse, where you can find out more about its history.

A minute down the road you'll find **King House,** a restored Georgian mansion

now home to a visitor centre (with some rather interesting mannequins on display to tell historical tales). There's a tearoom out in the courtyard, where they often hold markets or events at weekends – it's worth keeping an eye on their calendar to see what's on.

From Boyle, head south on the N61, turning right onto the R361 to make your way south, passing briefly through County Sligo until you're back in Roscommon. You're heading for **Clonalis House,** a home with over 1,500 years of heritage in its bones. It's owned (and lived in) by the O'Conor family, who are descendants of Ireland's last High Kings, and they open the house for guided tours between June and August, where they'll weave in their family story with the history of the estate. You can spend the night too, in the beautiful cottages they have on the grounds.

An ogham stone which forms the lintel of Oweynagat Cave, near Rathcroghan.

You'll pass through **Castlerea** as you aim for your next spot, which is a little off the beaten track. **Oweynagat Cave** may not seem like much to the naked eye, but it's the folklore around it that makes it interesting – this was once known as Ireland's gate to Hell, and where it was believed spirits would pass through on the eve of Samhain, what we know now as Halloween.

This little corner of the county is peppered with burial mounds too, which adds to the mythical aura around the green fields.

Next up, you'll pass back down through Roscommon, turning right off the N63 on the L1806. If you want to head back along the lake, you can turn off to **Portrunny Harbour**, to drive the waterside road and soak up the lake views.

Otherwise, stick to the N61, which will take you back to Athlone. First though, turn off to head briefly to **Hodson Bay** – there's a big hotel there that serves food,

and also **Baysports,** an adventure set-up on the lake where you can leap around the inflatable park, or rent kayaks for a more peaceful jaunt on the water.

Athlone is a ten-minute drive away, and here you can see the sights you missed on day one or head out for dinner – Thyme is a chef's favourite, and The Fatted Calf is great for hearty, meat-focused menu. You could also get more casual grub at Dead Centre Brewing, a microbrewery with tables on the river, and don't miss a drink in Sean's Bar, the oldest pub in Ireland.

Sean's Bar.

Church of
St Peter
and Paul.

LEINSTER (start) – Trip 25: 8 days
Highlights of Ireland

Sometimes you want a road trip to be purely scenic, the road taking you along soaring clifftops as the waves crash against the shore, or snaking along the edge of giant, calm lakes. But on other occasions, you want a road trip that'll get you from A to B as quickly as possible, so you can spend time out of the car and exploring the cities.

This road trip takes you from A to B, but also to C and D and ... well, you get the picture. This is the kind of trip that a visitor to Ireland would take in order to see as much of the country as possible in a relatively short period of time. You'll tick off Dublin, Kildare, Kilkenny, Waterford, Tipperary, Cork, Killarney, Limerick, Galway, Westport and Athlone, in roughly 8 days. That allows you a bit more time to experience each town or city properly, to visit the attractions and have a bit of downtime, too – after all, Ireland isn't a country to be rushed around. You might look at the driving time each day and think you're not spending much time behind the wheel, but if you go any faster you'll likely miss out (and be exhausted to boot).

While I've dubbed this drive the Highlights of Ireland, really what that means is the highlights of Irish cities and towns – while there are some scenic stretches, really this is about hitting the big spots. You could also choose to tag on some additional drives, and where that's a possibility, I've linked an option at the end of the day.

Need to Know

Duration: 8 days

Distance: 995km/618 miles

When to go: May or October

Start at: Dublin

Finish at: Dublin

Quick view

Day 1: Dublin to Waterford

Day 2: Waterford to Cork

Day 3: Cork to Killarney

Day 4: Killarney to Limerick

Day 5: Limerick to Galway

Day 6: Galway to Westport

Day 7: Westport to Athlone

Day 8: Athlone to Dublin

The route

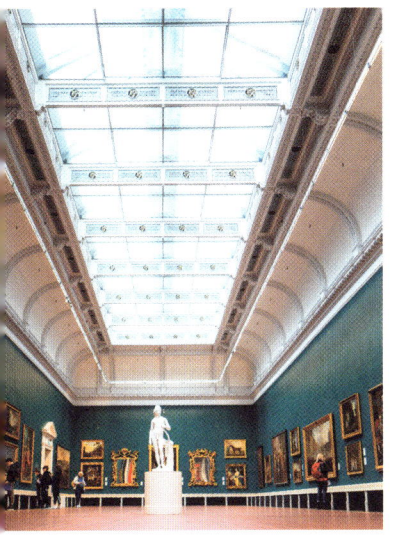

National Gallery of Ireland.

Day 1 – Dublin to Waterford

We'll start in **Dublin,** for no other reason than ease. But whether it's your first time in the city or you know it well, there's always something that should grab your attention – visit one of the National Museums, such as the **National Gallery of Ireland** or stroll around Stephen's Green or the Iveagh Gardens before you hit the road (see page 153 for other ideas).

There's definitely nothing scenic about the road out of Dublin – check the traffic to see which way is best, depending on when you're leaving – but in all likelihood you'll join the N7 from the M50, heading out into **Kildare.** If you'd like to, you can make a detour to see Newbridge Silver or The Curragh Racecourse, but otherwise you're sticking to the motorway all the way to **Kilkenny.**

Here, you can explore the castle, **Butler Gallery**, take a stroll around the **Medieval Mile** and keep an eye on the pavement, to catch glimpses of the famous fossils found in Kilkenny marble. If you want more time to explore, spend the night here, but if you're happy to crack on then

179

Rock of Cashel.

Waterford is less than an hour's drive away, on the M9.

Day 2 – Waterford to Cork

After some time exploring the city (see page 96), head out of town on the N24 to make your way through County Tipperary. There are a few beautiful stopping points – **Carrick-on-Suir** is a lovely town, and you'll also pass through **Clonmel** on your way up to see the **Rock of Cashel** (see page 86). Afterwards, head down to **Cahir**, a beautiful village with a castle at its heart – if you do have the time, the walk from the castle along the river to Swiss Cottage is a must.

From there, **Cork** city is roughly an hour's drive away, and your destination for the night. Check out the trad sessions

Blackrock Castle Observatory.

Ross Castle in Killarney National Park.

in the local pubs, or head to Marina Market for street food in a former warehouse building.

Optional add-on: Day 2 of Copper Coast and East Cork.

Day 3 – Cork to Killarney

Now, there's not much driving in this day at all, so you could opt to speed through and head to **Limerick** today as well. But realistically, you'll want time to see both **Cork** city (see page 96) and Killarney (see page 43). You'll almost certainly want to spend time in the **Killarney National Park,** because that's the big draw here – if you were really keen (and didn't spend much time out of the car) you could probably tag on the **Ring of Kerry drive.** But that takes the guts of four hours without stopping, so as an alternative, you could just drive out to park at Kate Kearney's Cottage and walk the **Gap of Dunloe,** or drive the scenic route to **Kenmare,** which takes around 45 minutes.

Optional add-on: Ring of Kerry.

Day 4 – Killarney to Limerick

How you spend the day here depends on what you'd like to see (and how much driving you're willing to do). You'll start in **Killarney** and end in **Limerick,** and if you were to drive straight with no distractions, you could knock it out in under two hours. However, you could choose to create your own adventure, and veer off course to drive t**he Wild Atlantic Way** up the coast, or head to **Dingle** to drive the beautiful **Slea Head** (see page 181). The latter would add at least three hours on to your total drive, not allowing for stops, but it's one hell of a road trip.

Optional add-on: Wild Atlantic Way.

Day 5: Limerick to Galway

Today's drive is even shorter, if you take the quick route. But do allow for some time in both **Limerick** (see page 85) and **Galway** (see page 13), both of which have plenty to see and do. However, if you'd like to spend more time driving and take

Lough Derg, County Tipperary.

the scenic route, you could drive the Wild Atlantic Way up to Galway, or even head east to see Lough Derg, via Tipperary. It doesn't add too much time to the total, but you'll get to see some of the Tipperary highlights along the way. Call in to see Nenagh Castle, and have some lunch at the cosy Larkins in Garrykennedy, where you can have a bowl of chowder by the fire. If you like a sauna, make a pit stop in Ritual in Dromineer.

Optional add-on: **Lough Derg** (see day one of Tipperary Highlights for inspiration).

Day 6 – Galway to Westport

Again, if you want to see both **Galway** city and **Westport** town (see page 77), you can drive the quick 90 minutes between the two, sticking to the main roads. But **Connemara** is right there and begging to be explored, so you could drive an amended version of the Galway to Connemara road trip (see page 12), sticking to the N59 and aiming for **Clifden,** passing through the gorgeous

landscapes of **Connemara National Park** on your way. You'll get to tick off **Killary Fjord**, too – it's a stunning drive.

But do allow a bit of time to appreciate **Westport** – it's one of the most charming

Clifden castle ruins.

Achill Island.

towns in Ireland, with an excellent food scene and loads of music flittering out of the pubs. If you only have time for one, make a beeline for Matt Molloy's.

Optional add-on: Connemara.

Day 7 – Westport to Athlone

Unfortunately, much of what makes County Mayo so special is to the north – the wild landscapes of Nephin, the windswept beauty of the north coast and

the otherworldly **Erris Peninsula** (see page 78. But you need to head back east, so unless you're playing with some extra time, you'll head straight out towards **Athlone** on a drive that'll take two hours without stopping.

If you do want an adventure beforehand, the easiest spot would be **Achill.** Drive out from Westport along the Wild Atlantic Way and make the bay of **Keem** your goal – it's often voted the

Wild Nephin National Park.

Westport bridge.

most beautiful beach in the world. You can potentially get there in about an hour and 15 minutes, but bear in mind you'll need to follow the same route back to get to Athlone. There, you can visit the castle (see page 171) and check out the local sights, and add on a bit of the Ireland's Hidden Heartlands route, if you like (see page 170). You could also just tag on a visit to **Clonmacnoise,** the monastic site that dates back to the sixth-century – it's a 30 minute drive from Athlone town (see page 172).

Optional add-on: Achill.

Day 8 – Athlone to Dublin

Now, if you wanted another option to speed up the trip and knock a night off, you could drive nonstop from **Westport** to **Dublin** in about three and a half hours, depending on traffic. But if you're sticking to the plan, the drive from Athlone to Dublin is well under two hours.

If you want to bring a bit of history and heritage into the trip, take a detour to **Brú na Bóinne,** to visit one of Ireland's most treasured sites (see page 146). It'll add about an hour onto your drive, and you'll need to allow at least three to four hours to see Newgrange, Knowth and the visitor centre. But it's a glorious end to a trip that ticks off all of Ireland's big hitters, wrapping up in an ancient tomb that's older than both Stonehenge and the Great Pyramids of Giza. Afterwards, you'll nip down the N2 and the M2 and be back in **Dublin** in just over an hour, ready to wrap up your road trip with a pint in O'Donoghue's, the Long Hall or Toners, for the cherry on top of a week seeing the best of Ireland.

Optional add-on: Brú na Bóinne.

Aerial view of Dublin and river Liffey.

Index

Picture credits

The publisher gratefully acknowledges the following image copyright holders. All images are copyright © individual rights holders unless stated otherwise. Every effort has been made to trace copyright holders, or copyright holders not mentioned here. If there have been any errors or omissions, the publisher would be happy to rectify this in any reprint.

6	Helen Hotson	58	Helen Hotson	102	Louiele	147	MN Studio
8	Dawid K Photography	59	Eli Bolyarska	103	Gabriel12	148	MN Studio
13	Mark Gusev	59	Patryk Kosmider	105	Natalie Hora	148	Fotogro
14	Robert Harding Video	61	John O Callaghan	106	Nahlik	149	Sphotomax
14	Junk Culture	62	Louielea	106	Kim Linda Casey	149	Ewy Media
15	Irina Ws	62	Jksz Photography	107	Stephen Barnes	150	Fotogro
16	Mark Gusev	63	Algirdas Gelazius	108	Ballygally View Images	151	Bjoern Alberts
16	Johannes Rigg	64	Timaldo	109	Adacquarica	153	Benoit Daoust/DT
17	Mark Gusev	64	Algirdas Gelazius	110	Dawid K Photography	154	Aart Jonkers
19	Milosz Maslanka	65	John O Callaghan	111	Ronniejcmc	155	Dawid K Photography
19	Lucky Team Studio	66	Kieran Hayes Photo	113	Dwbuick	156	365 Focus Photography
20	D J Kennedy Photo	66	Margaret111	114	Ballygally View Images	157	Bob Hilscher
21	Colin Mannion	67	Hugh O'Connor	115	Ballygally View Images	157	Chris Dorney
21	Bartlomiej Rybacki	67	Makasana Photo/DT	115	Helioscribe	158	Paul Briden
22	Elena Schweitzer	70	Makasana Photo/DT	116	Shawnwil23	159	Irish Drone Photography
23	Lukassek	71	Katjen	117	Helioscribe	159	Julian Gazzard
25	David Steele	72	Makasana Photo	118	Ondrej Prochazka	161	Emfa16
26	D. Ribeiro	73	Morrison	118	Adam Bialek	161	Al Kelly
26	Lyd Photography	74	Patryk Kosmider	119	John And Penny	162	Alex Romanjski
27	Charles Stewart	75	Ipics	121	Mick Harper	163	Vvlasovs
28	Lisandro Luis Trarbach	75	MN Studio	121	Northlight Photoart	163	2intour
29	Patryk Kosmider	76	Mark Gusev	122	Stephen Barnes	164	Irene Fox
30	Jonno Marshall	77	Robert Harding Video	122	Ballygally View Images	164	Andres Conema
31	Fotogro	78	Keith Levit	123	Adam Bialek	165	4h4 Ph
33	Lukassek	78	Photo Mom	124	Pics721	166	Inalex
34	Michael Gismo	79	Lukassek	125	Agaglowala	168	Tokar
35	Ian Mitchinson	79	Lukassek	127	Navorol Photograph	169	Tokar
36	Shawnwil 23	80	Fotogro	127	Wirestock Creators	171	Gabriela Insuratelu
37	4h4 Ph	84	Lukassek	128	Makasana Photo	172	Atelier2j
37	Patrick Mangan	84	Sarah Fahy Design	128	Gerry Mcnally	172	Yackers1
39	Ianmitchinson	85	Dvlcom	129	Ballygally View Images	173	4h4 Ph
40	Naeem Photographer	86	Pierre Leclerc	129	Irina Ws	174	Tokar
41	Paul Gibbons	86	Thomas Bresenhuber	130	Lyd Photography	175	Lukassek
43	Pierre Leclerc	87	Andrzej Bartyzel	130	Joaquin Ossorio Castillo	176	Cathalpeelo/Wikipedia
45	Patryk Kosmider	88	D. Ribeiro	131	John Clarke Photo	176	Remizov
45	Armin Binz	88	Jksz Photography	132	Sean Kelly Pix	177	Foto Para Ti
45	4h4 Ph	89	Roy Harris	134	Lukassek	179	Benoit Daoust
46	Carlos Sanchez Benayas	91	Fotogro	135	4kclips	180	Piotr Machowczyk
46	Teapot Press	91	Nicola K Photos	135	Lukassek	180	Mikemike10
47	Agaglowala	92	Michal Wlodarczyk	136	Paul Shiels	181	Gabriel12
49	Colin Mannion	93	Msjr1990	136	Lukassek	182	Lee Mullins
49	David Souto	93	Jorge Corcuera	137	Lukassek	182	Foto Para Ti
50	Gabriel12	94	Andrea Anci	139	Roberto Rizzi	183	Bartlomiej Rybacki
51	Luca Photo	95	Ronan McLaughlin	140	Avillfoto	183	Bonn Bonn foto
51	Lough Avalla Farm Loop	96	Madrugada Verde	140	Eimantas Juskevicius	184	Frank Bach
51	Chris Dorney	96	Artur Bogacki	141	Pavel Voitukovic	185	Alexey Fedorenko
52	Mark Gusev	97	Michalakis Ppalis	142	Remizov		
52	Domododragon	99	Xseon	142	MC Image		Maps: Base maps
53	Jon Sullivan/Wiki	99	Eanna Keenan	143	Jrp Studio		© maproom.net
55	Avillfoto	100	Shawnwil23	144	Irish Drone Photography		
56	Makasana Photo	100	Roy Harris	145	Rijksmuseum/Wikipedia		Routes: Ben Potter
56	Xamnesiacx84	101	Elena Elisseeva	146	Spectrumblue		
57	Bonn Bonn Foto	102	Cbiss	146	Kirk Gulden		

Photographers are from Shutterstock, unless stated otherwise. DT: Dreamstime.

T159/01/2-26/LV/PNB